# NOISES OFF

'Michael Frayn's new play is a farce about farce taking the clichés
of the genre, and shaking them inventively through a series of
kaleidoscopic patterns. Never missing a trick, it has as its first act
a *pastiche* of traditional farce; as its second, a contemporary
variant on the formula; as its third, an elaborate undermining of
it. The play opens with a touring company dress-rehearsing
*Nothing On,* a conventional farce. Mixing mockery and homage,
Frayn heaps into this play-within-a-play a hilarious melee of
stock characters and situations. Caricatures — cheery char,
outraged wife and squeaky blonde — stampede in and out of
doors. Voices rise and trousers fall . . . a farce that makes you
think as well as laugh.' Peter Kemp, *TLS.*

'A pulverisingly funny play' Michael Billington, *Guardian.*

'The funniest play on offer in London' Benedict Nightingale,
*New Statesman.*

'A great farce' James Fenton, *Sunday Times.*

'Mr Frayn's brilliant and best work' Jack Tinker, *Daily Mail.*

'The funniest play I have ever seen in the West End' Ned Chaillet,
*The Times.*

# Michael Frayn

# NOISES OFF

A play in three acts

METHUEN · LONDON

A Methuen Paperback

First published in Great Britain in 1982 as a Methuen Paperback
original by Methuen London Ltd, 11 New Fetter Lane,
London EC4P 4EE

Reprinted in this definitive, post-production version in 1983
by Methuen London Ltd

Set in IBM 10pt Journal by 🅰 Tek-Art, Croydon, Surrey
Printed in Great Britain by Richard Clay (The Chaucer Press) Ltd,
Bungay, Suffolk.

ISBN 0 413 50670 3

*Nothing On* programme compiled by Michael Frayn, Martin
Tickner and the Company. First published by Theatreprint.

## Author's Note

I am even more indebted to other people than usual with this play. I should particularly like to thank:

Martin Tickner, who commissioned the first short stage prototype, entitled *Exits,* for a midnight matinee of the Combined Theatrical Charities, at the Theatre Royal, Drury Lane, on 10 September 1977;
Eric Thompson, who navigated this strange craft, and Denis Quilley, Patricia Routledge, Edward Fox, Dinsdale Landen, and Polly Adams, who crewed it;
Michael Codron, who thereupon commissioned the full-length version, and waited for it with intermittent patience;
Scripts Ltd., of Gerrard St., who typed out the successive editions, with five different margins and (in Act Two) in two exactly synchronous columns, without complaint;
Michael Blakemore, whose help with the text went well beyond what any author could reasonably expect of his director, and whose ideas are freely incorporated in the following pages.

*Noises Off* was first presented, by arrangement with Michael Codron, at the Lyric Theatre, Hammersmith, on 23 February 1982, and on 31 March by Michael Codron at the Savoy Theatre, London, with the following cast:

| | |
|---|---|
| DOTTY OTLEY | Patricia Routledge |
| LLOYD DALLAS | Paul Eddington |
| GARRY LEJEUNE | Nicky Henson |
| BROOKE ASHTON | Rowena Roberts |
| POPPY NORTON-TAYLOR | Yvonne Antrobus |
| FREDERICK FELLOWES | Tony Mathews |
| BELINDA BLAIR | Jan Waters |
| TIM ALLGOOD | Roger Lloyd Pack |
| SELSDON MOWBRAY | Michael Aldridge |
| ELECTRICIAN | Ray Edwards |

*Directed by* Michael Blakemore
*Designed by* Michael Annals
*Lighting by* Spike Gaden

ACT ONE: The living-room of the Brents' country home. Wednesday afternoon.

(Grand Theatre, Weston-Super-Mare, Monday, January 14th)

ACT ONE: The living-room of the Brents' country home. Wednesday afternoon.

(Theatre Royal, Goole. Wednesday matinee, February 13th)

ACT ONE: The living-room of the Brents' country home. Wednesday afternoon.

(Municipal Theatre, Stockton-on-Tees, Saturday, April 6th)

*The cast of* Noises Off *are performing a play called* Nothing On, *an extract from the programme of which follows.*

# Grand Theatre

## WESTON-SUPER-MARE

*Proprietors:* GRAND THEATRE (Weston-super-Mare) LIMITED
General Manager: E. E. A. GRADSHAW

The Grand Theatre
Weston-super-Mare
is a Member of the
Grand Group

Commencing Tuesday 15th January for One Week Only

**Otstar Productions Ltd**

Evenings at 7.45

*present*

Matinee: Wednesday
at 2.30

# DOTTY OTLEY

Saturday at 5.00
and 8.30

# BELINDA BLAIR

# GARRY LEJEUNE

*in*

# NOTHING ON

*by*

**ROBIN HOUSEMONGER**

*with*

**SELSDON MOWBRAY**
**BROOKE ASHTON**
**FREDERICK FELLOWES**

Directed by **LLOYD DALLAS**

Designed by **GINA STAIRWELL**

Lighting by
**CHUCK SPANNER**

Costumes by
**PATSY BUTTON**

WORLD PREMIERE PRIOR TO NATIONAL TOUR!

# Behind
# The Dressing Room Doors

**DOTTY OTLEY** makes a welcome return to the stage to create the role of Mrs. Clackett after playing Mrs. Hackett, Britain's most famous lollipop lady ('Ooh, I can't 'ardly 'old me lolly up!') in over 320 episodes of TV's ON THE ZEBRAS. She was born in Malta, the only daughter of Lt.Cdr. Clive Otley, R.N., D.S.M., and trained at the Estelle Birkwood School of Drama and Allied Arts, winning the Bronze Medal, and going on to the Embassy Theatre, Swiss Cottage, where she gained invaluable experience as ASM in successful productions like AS YOU DESIRE and STARCHED APRONS. Understudying Bee Duffell in HADDOCK'S EYES at the New Lindsey Theatre, Notting Hill Gate, and Margaret Lockwood in PETER PAN at the Scala, was followed by The King's Theatre, Peebles for a season, and then the Duke's Players at Lyme Regis for the better part of two seasons, and this in turn led to a prolonged stay in Australia, where she enjoyed some of the biggest successes of her career. When she gets the time she intends writing her memoirs, she says.

**BELINDA BLAIR** (Flavia Brent) has been on the stage since the age of four, when she made her debut in SINBAD THE SAILOR at the old Croydon Hippodrome as one of Miss Toni Tanner's Ten Tapping Tots. She subsequently danced her way round this country, Southern Africa, and the Far East in shows like ZIPPEDY-DOO-DA! and HERE COMES LES GIRLS! A damaged tendon led to her first straight parts in GOOD TIME GIRL, LADIES OF THE NIGHT, and RING TWICE FOR RITA. More recently she has been seen in such comedy hits as DON'T MR. DUDDLE!, WHO'S BEEN SLEEPING IN MY BED?, and TWICE TWO IS SEX. She is married to scriptwriter Terry Wough, who has contributed lead-in material to most of TV's chat shows. They have two sons and three retrievers.

**GARRY LEJEUNE** (Roger Tramplemain) was twice winner of the Rose Bruford Medal for Effort. His many successful tours have brought him to Weston-super-Mare only once before, when he was starring in THE ADVENTURES OF A WINDOW DRESSER. He has made innumerable television appearances, but is perhaps best-known as 'Cornetto', the ice-cream salesman who stirs the hearts of all the lollipop ladies in ON THE ZEBRAS. Recently made his 'big screen' debut in UP THE VIRGIN SOLDIERS, for which he was nominated as Best Male Newcomer under Forty in any British Low-Budget Comedy Film by readers of the SUN newspaper.

**SELSDON MOWBRAY** (Burglar) first 'trod the boards' in A MIDSUMMER NIGHT'S DREAM with the Ben Greet Players, with whom he toured for three years, playing, among other roles, Moth, Mustardseed, and Nerissa (!) After war service in the Artists' Rifles, outstanding seasons with various repertory companies across the length and breadth of Great Britain led to his first West End play, KELLY'S EYE. Then 'alfresco' in Regent's Park for several seasons, playing leads. To Stratford thence for Mercutio, King John, and the Porter in MACBETH. To Hollywood for several good supporting Roles, including Stand-In to Robert Newton. Back home he played King Lear in Portsmouth, and joined the BBC Rep for two months in 1938. Great War No. Two saw him back in Khaki. Invalided out in 1940 he continued to serve by joining Ensa, and performing all over the world in many different 'Theatres of War'. To Dublin in 1946, where he set up his own touring company playing the Classics, and rivalling the great Agnew Macmaster. Returned to England in 1952 and set up his own tour – a revival of MR. CINDERS. Since then, apart from an occasional excursion to 'tread the green', he has been busy writing his autobiography, which he is thinking of titling HANGING ON THE WALL.

# NOTHING ON

## by ROBIN HOUSEMONGER

Cast in order of appearance:

| | |
|---|---|
| Mrs Clackett | **DOTTY OTLEY** |
| Roger Tramplemain | **GARRY LEJEUNE** |
| Vicki | **BROOKE ASHTON** |
| Philip Brent | **FREDERICK FELLOWES** |
| Flavia Brent | **BELINDA BLAIR** |
| Burglar | **SELSDON MOWBRAY** |
| Sheikh | **FREDERICK FELLOWES** |

The action takes place in the living-room of the Brents' country home,
on a Wednesday afternoon

### for OTSTAR PRODUCTIONS LTD

| | |
|---|---|
| Company and Stage Manager | **TIM ALLGOOD** |
| Assistant Stage Manager | **POPPY NORTON-TAYLOR** |

---

**Production credits**
Sardines by Sardine Services. Miss Ashton's lenses by Double Vision Optical Ltd. Antique silverware and cardboard boxes by Mrs J. G. H. Norton-Taylor. Stethoscope and hospital trolley by Severn Surgical Supplies. Straitjacket by Kumfy Restraints Ltd. Coffins by G. Ashforth and Sons.

---

We gratefully acknowledge the generous support of EUROPEAN BREWERIES in sponsoring this production.

**BROOKE ASHTON** (Vicki) is probably best known as the girl wearing nothing but 'good, honest, natural froth' in the Hauptbahnhofbrau lager commercial. But she has enjoyed a flourishing stage career, extending from a widely acclaimed Dandini in Hull to six months in the Lebanon with PIXIE PEARLS. Her television appearances range from Girl at Infants' School in ON THE ZEBRAS to Girl in Strip Joint in ON PROBATION. Cinemagoers saw her in THE GIRL IN ROOM 14, where she played the Girl in Room 312.

**FREDERICK FELLOWES** (Philip Brent) comes from a theatrical family – his parents were a popular speciality dance act of the thirties and forties, 'The Funny Fellowes'. He taught at a prep school near Hayward's Heath before bowing to family tradition and joining the Osmosis Players. There followed successful seasons in Nairobi, Ventnor, and Southwold, and he was most recently seen in the controversial all-male version of THE TROJAN WOMEN. He is happily married, and lives near Crawley, where his wife breeds pedigree dogs. 'If she ever leaves me,' he says, 'it will probably be for an Irish wolfhound!'

**ROBIN HOUSEMONGER** (Author) was born in Worcester Park, Surrey, into a family 'unremarkable in every way except for an aunt with red hair who used to sing all the high twiddly bits from THE MERRY WIDOW over the tea-table.' He claims to have been the world's most unsuccessful gents hosiery wholesaler, and began writing 'to fill the long hours between one hosiery order and the next.' He turned this experience into his very first play, SOCKS BEFORE MARRIAGE, which ran in the West End for nine years. Several subsequent plays have been produced, and at least one of them broke box office records in Perth, Western Australia. NOTHING ON is his seventeenth play.

**LLOYD DALLAS** (Director) 'read English at Cambridge, and stagecraft at the Salisbury.' A Commonwealth Scholarship took him to Princeton, where he spent his time 'commuting to New York to see Miller and musicals on Broadway, and Lee Strasberg and Tallulah Bankhead at a party on East 10th St.' Since then Lloyd has directed plays 'in most parts of Britain,' winning the South of Scotland Critics' Circle Special Award in 1968. In 1972 he directed a highly successful season for the National Theatre of Sri Lanka. In recent years Lloyd has probably become best-known for his brilliant series of 'Shakespeare in Summer' productions in the parks of the inner London boroughs.

**TIM ALLGOOD** (Company Stage Manager) trained for a career in Market Research, and became interested in the theatre only through a chance holiday visit to a local production of THERE'S A GIRL IN MY SOUP. He had got himself taken on by the company as Assistant Stage Manager before he realised that the girl in question was not only in the soup, but also married, with two growing children! During a production of HAMLET at the Lyceum, Portsmouth, he took over the part of Polonius at short notice, but subsequently found himself more in demand on the technical side. His most recent job was with BETROTHED, a thriller by Sam Brennicle, both on the tour prior to its West End opening in December 1980, and again on the tour which followed the conclusion of its successful West End run in January 1981.

**POPPY NORTON-TAYLOR** (Assistant Stage Manager) is from a family found more often on the Boards of leading companies than on the boards with touring companies. Her father is chairman of European Breweries, but has been 'terribly sweet about it all – so far!' After schools in Cheltenham and Montreux she found life far too full to leave time for work. So this is her first job and she is enjoying the challenge enormously. Her hobbies include riding, ski-ing, tennis, reading good books, and loving anything small and furry.

**ACT ONE**

*The living-room of the Brents' country home. Wednesday
afternoon. (Grand Theatre, Weston-Super-Mare, Monday
January 14.)*

*A delightful 16th-century posset mill, 25 miles from
London. Lovingly converted, old-world atmosphere, many
period features. Fully equipped with every aid to modern
living, and beautifully furnished throughout by owner
now resident abroad. Ideal for overseas company seeking
perfect English setting to house senior executive. Minimum
three months let. Apply sole agents: Squire, Squire,
Hackham and Dudley.*

*THE ACCOMMODATION COMPRISES: an open-plan
living area, with a staircase leading to a gallery. A notable
feature is the extensive range of entrances and exits
provided. On the ground floor the front door gives access
to the mature garden and delightful village beyond. Another
door leads to the elegant panelled study, and a third to
the light and airy modern service quarters. A fourth door
opens into a luxurious bathroom/WC suite, and a full-length
south-facing window affords extensive views. On the
gallery level is the door to the master bedroom, and another
to a small but well-proportioned linen cupboard. A
corridor gives access to all the other rooms in the upper
parts of the house. Another beautifully equipped
bathroom/WC suite opens off the landing halfway up the
stairs.*

*All in all, a superb example of the traditional English
set-builder's craft — a place where the discerning theatre-
goer will feel instantly at home.*

*As the curtain rises, the award-winning modern
telephone is ringing.*

*Enter from the service quarters* MRS CLACKETT, *a housekeeper of character. She is carrying an imposing plate of sardines.*

MRS CLACKETT. It's no good you going on. I can't open sardines *and* answer the phone. I've only got one pair of feet. (*Puts the sardines down on the telephone table by the sofa, and picks up the phone.*) Hello . . . Yes, but there's no one here, love . . . No, Mr Brent's not here . . . He lives here, yes, but he don't live here now because he lives in Spain . . . Mr Philip Brent, that's right . . . The one who writes the plays, that's him, only now he writes them in Spain . . . No, she's in Spain, too, they're all in Spain, there's no one here . . . Am I in Spain? No, I'm not in Spain, dear. I look after the house for them, only I go home at one o'clock on Wednesday, so that's where *I* am . . . No, because I've got a nice plate of sardines to put my feet up with, and they've got colour here, and it's the royal what's it called — the royal you know — where's the paper, then . . . ?

*She searches in the newspaper.*

. . . And if it's to do with letting the house then you'll have to ring the house-agents, because they're the agents for the house . . . Squire, Squire, Hackham and who's the other one . . . ? No, they're not in Spain, they're next to the phone in the study. Squire, Squire, Hackham, and hold on, I'll go and look.

*She replaces the receiver.*

*Or so the stage-direction says in Robin Housemonger's play,* Nothing On. *In fact, though, she puts the receiver down beside the phone instead.*

Always the same, isn't it. Soon as you take the weight off your feet, down it all comes on your head.

*Exit* MRS CLACKETT *into the study, still holding the newspaper.*

*Or so the stage-direction says. In fact she moves off holding the plate of sardines instead of the newspaper. As she does so,* DOTTY OTLEY, *the actress who is playing the part of* MRS CLACKETT, *comes out of character to comment on the move.*

DOTTY. And I take the sardines. No, I leave the sardines. No, I *take* the sardines.

*The disembodied voice of* LLOYD DALLAS, *the director of* Nothing On, *replies from somewhere out in the darkness of the auditorium.*

LLOYD. You leave the sardines, and you put the receiver back.

DOTTY. Oh yes, I put the receiver back.

*She puts the receiver back, and moves off again with the sardines.*

LLOYD. And you leave the sardines.

DOTTY. And I *leave* the sardines?

LLOYD. You *leave* the sardines.

DOTTY. I put the receiver back and I leave the sardines.

LLOYD. Right.

DOTTY. We've changed that, have we, love?

LLOYD. No, love.

DOTTY. That's what I've always been doing?

LLOYD. I shouldn't say that, Dotty, my precious.

DOTTY. How about the words, love? Am I getting some of them right?

LLOYD. Some of them have a very familiar ring.

DOTTY. Only it's like a fruit machine in there.

LLOYD. I know that, Dotty.

DOTTY. I open my mouth, and I never know if it's going to come out three oranges or two lemons and a banana.

LLOYD. Anyway, it's not midnight yet. We don't open till tomorrow. So you're holding the receiver . . .

DOTTY. I'm holding the receiver . . .

LLOYD. 'Squire, Squire, Hackham, and hold on . . .'

DOTTY *resumes her performance as* MRS CLACKETT.

> MRS CLACKETT. Squire, Squire, Hackham, and hold on, don't go away, I'm putting it down.
>
> *She replaces the receiver.*
>
> Always the same, isn't it. Put your feet up for two minutes, and immediately they come running after you.
>
> *Exit* MRS CLACKETT *into the study, still holding the newspaper.*

*Only she isn't holding the newspaper.*

> *The sound of a key in the lock.*

LLOYD. Hold it.

> *The front door opens. On the doorstep stands* ROGER, *holding a cardboard box. He is about thirty, and has the well-appointed air of a man who handles high-class real estate.*
>
> ROGER. . . . my housekeeper, yes, but this is her afternoon off.

LLOYD. Hold it, Garry. Dotty!

> *Enter* VICKI *through the front door. She is a desirable property in her early twenties, well-built and beautifully maintained throughout.*
>
> ROGER. So we've got the place entirely to ourselves.

LLOYD. Hold it, Brooke. Dotty!

*Enter* DOTTY *from the study.*

DOTTY. Come back?

LLOYD. Yes, and go out again with the *newspaper*.

DOTTY. The newspaper? Oh, the newspaper.

LLOYD. You put the receiver back, you leave the sardines, and you go out with the newspaper.

GARRY. Here you are, love.

DOTTY. Sorry, love.

GARRY (*embraces her*). Don't worry, love. It's only the technical.

LLOYD. It's the dress, Garry, honey. It's the dress rehearsal.

GARRY. So when was the technical?

LLOYD. So when's the dress? We open tomorrow!

GARRY. Well, we're all thinking of it as the technical. (*To DOTTY:*) Aren't we, love?

DOTTY. It's all those words, my sweetheart.

GARRY. Don't worry about the words, Dotty, my pet.

DOTTY. Coming up like oranges and lemons.

GARRY. Listen, Dotty, your words are fine, your words are better than the, do you know what I mean? (*To BROOKE:*) Isn't that right?

BROOKE. Sorry?

GARRY (*to DOTTY*). I mean, OK, so he's the, you know. Fine. But, Dotty, love, you've been playing this kind of part for, well, I mean, Jesus, Dotty, you know what I mean.

LLOYD. All right? So Garry and Brooke are off, Dotty's holding the receiver . . .

GARRY. No, but here we are, we're all thinking, my God, we open tomorrow, we've only had a fortnight to rehearse, we don't know where we are, but my God, here we are!

DOTTY. That's right, my sweet. Isn't that right, Lloyd?

LLOYD. Beautifully put, Garry.

GARRY. No, but I mean, we've got to play Weston-super-Mare all the rest of this week, then Yeovil, then God knows where, then God knows where else, and so on for God knows how long, and we're all of us feeling pretty much, you know . . . (*To BROOKE:*) I mean, aren't *you*?

BROOKE. Sorry?

LLOYD. Anyway, you're off, Dotty's holding the receiver . . .

GARRY. Sorry, Lloyd. But sometimes you just have to come right out with it. You know?

LLOYD. I know.

GARRY. Thanks, Lloyd.

LLOYD. OK, Garry. So you're off . . .

GARRY. Lloyd, let me just say one thing. Since we've stopped. I've worked with a lot of directors, Lloyd. Some of them were geniuses. Some of them were bastards. But I've never met one who was so totally and absolutely . . . I don't know . . .

LLOYD. Thank you, Garry. I'm very touched. Now will you get off the fucking stage?

*Exit GARRY through the front door.*

And, Brooke . . .

BROOKE. Yes?

LLOYD. Are you in?

BROOKE. In?

LLOYD. Are you there?

BROOKE. What?

LLOYD. You're out. OK. I'll call again. And on we go.

*Exit BROOKE through the front door.*

So there you are, holding the receiver.

DOTTY. So there I am, holding the receiver. I put the receiver back and I leave the sardines.

MRS CLACKETT. Always the same story, isn't it . . .

LLOYD. And you take the newspaper.

*She comes back, and picks up the newspaper and the receiver.*

DOTTY. I leave the sardines, I take the newspaper.

MRS CLACKETT. Always the same story, isn't it. It's a weight off your mind, it's a load off your stomach.

DOTTY. And off at last I go.

LLOYD. Leaving the receiver.

*She replaces the receiver and goes off into the study.*
*Enter* ROGER *as before, with the cardboard box.*

ROGER. . . . my housekeeper, yes, but this is her afternoon
off.

*Enter* VICKI *as before.*

So we've got the place entirely to ourselves.

ROGER *goes back and brings in a flight bag, and closes*
*the front door.*

I'll just check.

*He opens the door to the service quarters.* VICKI *gazes*
*round.*

Hello? Anyone at home?

*Closes the door.*

No, there's no one here. So what do you think?

VICKI. Great. And this is all yours?

ROGER. Just a little shack in the woods, really. Converted
posset mill. Sixteenth-century.

VICKI. It must have cost a bomb.

ROGER. Well, one has to have somewhere to entertain
one's business associates. Someone coming at four
o'clock, in fact. Arab. Oil. You know.

VICKI. Right. And I've got to get those files to our
Basingstoke office by four.

ROGER. Yes, we'll only just manage to fit it in. I mean,
we'll only just do it. I mean . . .

VICKI. Right, then.

ROGER (*puts down the box and opens the flight bag*). We
won't bother to chill the champagne.

VICKI. All these doors.

ROGER. Oh, only a handful, really. Study. Kitchens, and a
self-contained service flat for the housekeeper.

VICKI. Terrific. And which one's the . . .?

ROGER. What?

VICKI. You know . . .

ROGER. Oh. Through here.

*Opens the downstairs bathroom for her.*

VICKI. Fantastic.

*Exit* VICKI *into the bathroom.*
*Enter* MRS CLACKETT *from the study, without the newspaper.*

MRS CLACKETT. Now I've lost the sardines . . .

*Mutual surprise.* ROGER *closes the door to the bathroor and slips the champagne back into the bag.*

ROGER. I'm sorry. I thought there was no one here.

MRS CLACKETT. I'm not here. I'm off, only it's the royal you know, where they wear those hats, and they're all covered in fruit, and who are you?

ROGER. I'm from the agents.

MRS CLACKETT. From the agents?

ROGER. Squire, Squire, Hackham and Dudley.

MRS CLACKETT. Oh. Which one are you, then? Squire, Squire, Hackham, or Dudley?

ROGER. I'm Tramplemain.

MRS CLACKETT. Walking in here as if you owned the place! I thought you was a burgular.

ROGER. No, I just dropped in to . . . go into a few things. Well, to check some of the measurements, do one or two odd jobs.

*The bathroom door opens.* ROGER *closes it.*

Oh, and a client. I'm showing a prospective tenant over the house.

VICKI (*off, opening the door*): What's wrong with this door?

ROGER. She's thinking of renting it. Her interest is definitely aroused.

*Enter* VICKI *from bathroom.*

VICKI. That's not the bedroom.

ROGER. The bedroom? No, that's the downstairs bathroom and WC suite. And this is the housekeeper. Mrs Crockett.

MRS CLACKETT. Clackett, dear, Clackett.

VICKI. Oh. Hi.

ROGER. She's not really here.

MRS CLACKETT. Only it's the colour.

ROGER. It's the royal, you know.

MRS CLACKETT. It's black-and-white at home.

ROGER (*to* MRS CLACKETT): Don't worry about us.

MRS CLACKETT (*picks up the sardines*). I'll have the sound on low.

ROGER. We'll just inspect the house.

MRS CLACKETT. Only now I've lost the newspaper.

*Exit* MRS CLACKETT *into the study, carrying the sardines.*

*Only she leaves them behind.*

LLOYD. Sardines!

ROGER. I'm sorry about this.

LLOYD. Sardines!

VICKI. That's all right. We don't want the television, do we?

LLOYD. Sardines!

*Enter* DOTTY *from the study.*

DOTTY. I've forgotten the sardines.

GARRY. Lloyd! These bloody sardines! We've got to do something about them. We can't go on like this.

LLOYD. Can't go on like what, Garry?

GARRY. OK, it's all right for you, sitting out there, but we've got to *work* with these sardines, we all feel the same. (*To* BROOKE:) Don't we?

BROOKE. Sorry?

GARRY. The sardines.

BROOKE. What sardines?

GARRY (*to* LLOYD). I mean, we're up here, working our backsides off, and there are four plates of sardines coming on in Act One alone. Do you know what I mean?

LLOYD. Poppy! (*To* GARRY:) You want something instead of the sardines? Is that what you're saying? You want Poppy to mash up some banana?

DOTTY. We don't want four plates of mashed banana.

*Enter* POPPY, *the assistant stage manager, from the wings.*

LLOYD. Poppy, we're changing the sardines.

GARRY. We're not getting at you, Poppy, love.

DOTTY. We think the sardines are lovely.

GARRY (*to* DOTTY). I'd be perfectly happy with the sardines if you were happy with them, love.

DOTTY. I'm happy with them if you're happy with them, love.

LLOYD. So, Garry, honey, what exactly are you saying?

GARRY. What we're saying, Lloyd, is simply this: here we are busting our guts up here and, *Christ!*

LLOYD. I see. Got that, Poppy?

POPPY. Um. Well.

LLOYD. Right. On we go. From Dotty's exit. And, Poppy . . .

POPPY. Yes?

LLOYD. Don't let this happen again.

POPPY. Oh. No.

*Exit* POPPY *into the wings.*

GARRY. Sorry, Lloyd. I thought we ought to get that straight.

LLOYD. Of course. As long as Dotty's happy.

DOTTY. Absolutely happy, Lloyd, my love.

LLOYD. Will you do something for me, then, Dotty, my precious?

DOTTY. Anything, Lloyd, my sweet.

LLOYD. Take the sardines off with you.

> *Exit* MRS CLACKETT *into study, carrying the sardines.*

ROGER. I'm sorry about this.

VICKI. That's all right. We don't want the television, do we?

ROGER. Only she's been in the family for generations.

VICKI. Great. Come on, then. (*Starts upstairs.*) I've got
to be in Basingstoke by four.

ROGER. Perhaps we should just have a glass of champagne.

VICKI. We'll take it up with us.

ROGER. Yes. Well . . .

VICKI. And don't let my files out of sight.

ROGER. No. Only . . .

VICKI. What?

ROGER. Well . . .

VICKI. Her?

ROGER. She has been in the family for generations.

> *Enter* MRS CLACKETT *from the study, with the
> newspaper but without the sardines.*

MRS CLACKETT. Sardines . . . Sardines . . . It's not for me
to say, of course, dear, only I will just say this: don't
think twice about it — take the plunge. You'll really
enjoy it here.

VICKI. Oh. Great.

MRS CLACKETT (*to* ROGER): Won't she, love?

ROGER. Yes. Well. Yes!

MRS CLACKETT (*to* VICKI): And we'll enjoy having you. (*To* ROGER:) Won't we, love?

ROGER. Oh. Well.

VICKI. Terrific.

MRS CLACKETT. Sardines, sardines. Can't put your feet up on an empty stomach, can you.

*Exit* MRS CLACKETT *to service quarters.*

VICKI. You see? She thinks it's great. She's even making us sardines!

ROGER. Well . . .

VICKI. I think she's terrific.

ROGER. Terrific.

VICKI. So which way?

ROGER (*picks up the bags*). All right. Before she comes back with the sardines.

VICKI. Up here?

ROGER. Yes, yes.

VICKI. In here?

ROGER. Yes, yes, yes.

*Exeunt* ROGER *and* VICKI *into mezzanine bathroom.*

VICKI. It's another bathroom.

*They reappear.*

ROGER. No, no, no.

VICKI. Always trying to get me into bathrooms.

ROGER. I mean in *here.*

*Nods at the next door — the first along the gallery.* VICKI *leads the way in.* ROGER *follows.*

VICKI. Oh, black sheets! (*Produces one.*)

ROGER. It's the airing cupboard (*Throws the sheet back.*) This one, this one, this one.

*He drops the bag and box and struggles nervously to open the second door along the gallery, the bedroom.*

VICKI. Oh, you're in a real state!

ROGER. Come on, then.

VICKI. You can't even get the door open.

*Exeunt ROGER and VICKI into the bedroom.*

*Only they can't, because the bedroom door won't open.*

*The sound of a key in the lock, and the front door opens. On the doorstep stands PHILIP, carrying a cardboard box. He is in his forties, with a deep suntan, and writes attractive new plays with a charming period atmosphere.*

PHILIP.  . . . Yes, but then this is Mrs Clackett's afternoon off.

LLOYD. Hold it.

*Enter FLAVIA. She is in her thirties, the perfect companion piece to the above.*

LLOYD. Hold it.

PHILIP. We've got the place entirely to ourselves.

*PHILIP brings in a flight bag and closes the door.*

*Only the door won't stay closed. A pause, while GARRY struggles to open the door upstairs, and FREDERICK struggles to close the door downstairs.*

LLOYD. And God said, Hold it. And they held it. And God saw that it was terrible.

GARRY (*to FREDERICK and BELINDA, the actor and actress playing PHILIP and FLAVIA*). Sorry, loves, the door won't open.

BELINDA. Sorry, love, this door won't close.

LLOYD. And God said, Poppy!

FREDERICK. Sorry, everyone. Am I doing something wrong? You know how stupid I am about doors.

BELINDA. Freddie, my sweet, you're doing it perfectly.

FREDERICK. As long as it's not me that's broken it.

*Enter* POPPY *from the wings.*

LLOYD. And there was Poppy. And God said, Be fruitful and multiply, and fetch Tim to fix the doors.

*Exit* POPPY *into the wings.*

BELINDA. Oh, I love technicals!

GARRY. She loves technicals! (*Fondly.*) Isn't she just, I mean, Christ, she loves technicals! Dotty! Where's Dotty?

BELINDA. Everyone's always so nice to everyone.

GARRY. Oh! Isn't she just, I mean, she really is, isn't she.

*Enter* DOTTY *from the service quarters.*

(*To* DOTTY:) Belinda's being all, you know.

BELINDA (*holding out an arm to* FREDERICK). But Freddie, my precious, don't you like a nice all-night technical?

FREDERICK. The only thing I like about technicals is you get a chance to sit on the furniture.

*He sits.*

BELINDA. Oh, Freddie, my precious! It's lovely to see you cheering up and making jokes.

*She sits beside him, and embraces him.*

FREDERICK. Oh, was that a joke?

BELINDA. This is such a lovely company to work with. It's such a happy company.

DOTTY. Wait till we've got to Stockton-on-Tees in twelve weeks' time.

BELINDA (*sits*). Are *you* all right, Lloyd, my precious?

LLOYD. I'm starting to know what God felt like when he sat out there in the darkness creating the world. (*Takes a pill.*)

BELINDA. What did he feel like, Lloyd, my love?

LLOYD. Very pleased he'd taken his Valium.

BELINDA. He had six days, of course. We've only got six hours.

LLOYD. And God said, Where the hell is Tim?

*Enter from the wings* TIM, *the company stage manager. He is exhausted.*

And there the hell *was* Tim. And God said, Let there be doors, that open when they open, and close when they close, and let the doors divide the world which is in front of the set from the world which is behind the set.

TIM. Do something?

LLOYD. Doors.

TIM. I was getting the bananas. For the sardines.

LLOYD. Doors.

TIM. Doors?

LLOYD. I bet God had a stage manager who understood English, too.

BELINDA. Tim, my love, this door won't close.

GARRY. And the bedroom won't, you know.

TIM. Oh, right. (*Sets to work on the doors.*)

BELINDA (*to* LLOYD). He hasn't been to bed for forty-eight hours.

LLOYD. Don't worry, Tim. Only another twenty-four hours, and it'll be the end of the day.

LLOYD *comes up on stage.*

BELINDA. Oh, look, he's come down on earth amongst us.

LLOYD. Listen. Since we've stopped anyway. OK, it took two days to get the set up, so we shan't have time for a dress rehearsal. Don't worry. Think of the first night as a dress rehearsal. If we can just get through the play once tonight for doors and sardines. That's what it's all about. Doors and sardines. Getting on — getting off. Getting the sardines on — getting the sardines off. That's farce. That's the theatre. That's life.

BELINDA. Oh God, Lloyd, you're so deep.

LLOYD. So just keep going. Bang, bang, bang. Bang you're on. Bang you've said it. Bang you're off. And everything will be perfectly where's Selsdon?

BELINDA. Oh God.

GARRY. Oh God oh God oh God.

BELINDA. Selsdon!

GARRY. Selsdon!

LLOYD. Poppy!

DOTTY (*to* LLOYD). I thought he was in front, with you?

LLOYD. I thought he was round the back, with you?

*Enter* POPPY *from the wings.*

Is Mr Mowbray in his dressing-room?

*Exit* POPPY *into the wings.*

FREDERICK. Oh, I don't think he would. Not at a technical. (*To* BROOKE:) Would he?

BROOKE. Would who?

GARRY. Selsdon. We can't find him!

FREDERICK. I'm sure he wouldn't. Not at a technical.

DOTTY. Half a chance, he would.

BROOKE. Would what?

GARRY, DOTTY *and* LLOYD *make gestures to her of tipping a glass, or raising the elbow, or screwing the nose.*

BELINDA. Now come on, my sweets, be fair! We don't know.

FREDERICK. Let's not jump to any conclusions.

LLOYD. Let's just get the understudy dressed. Tim!

TIM. Yes?

LLOYD. Hurry up with those doors. You're going on for Selsdon.

TIM. Oh. Right.

DOTTY. He shouldn't have been out of sight! I said, he must never be out of sight!

BELINDA. He's been as good as gold all the way through rehearsals.

GARRY. Yes, because in the rehearsal room it was all, I don't know, but there we were, do you know what I mean?

LLOYD. You mean you could see everyone.

GARRY. And here it's all, you know.

LLOYD. Split into two. There's a front and a back. And instantly we've lost him.

*Enter* POPPY *from the wings.*

POPPY. He's not in his dressing-room.

DOTTY. You've looked in the lavatories?

POPPY. Yes.

DOTTY. And the scenery dock and the prop room and the paint store?

POPPY. Yes.

FREDERICK (*to* DOTTY). You've worked with him before, of course.

LLOYD (*to* POPPY). Ring the police.

*Exit* POPPY *into the wings.*

(*To* TIM:) Finished the doors? Right, get the gear on.

*Exit* TIM *into the wings.*
*Enter* SELSDON MOWBRAY *from the back of the stalls. He is in his seventies, and is wearing his burglar gear. He comes down the aisle during the following dialogue, and stands in front of the stage, watching everyone on it.*

I'm sorry, Dotty, my love.

DOTTY. No, it's my fault, Lloyd, my love.

LLOYD. I cast him.

DOTTY. 'Let's give him one last chance,' I said. 'One last chance!' I mean, what can you do? We were in weekly rep together in Peebles.

GARRY (*to* DOTTY): It's my fault, my precious — I shouldn't have let you. I should have put my foot down. I should have said, 'Look, Dotty, my darling, you simply cannot let your heart rule your, you know, because Dotty, my sweetheart, for you this tour isn't just, do you know what I mean? — This is your life savings!'

LLOYD. We know that, Garry, love.

BELINDA *puts a hand on* DOTTY's *arm.*

DOTTY. I'm not trying to make my fortune.

FREDERICK. Of course you're not, Dotty.

BELINDA. We know that.

DOTTY. I just wanted to put a little something by.

BELINDA. We know, love.

GARRY. Just something to buy a little house that she could I mean Jesus, that's not so much to ask.

BELINDA (*to* BROOKE): Now come on, my sweet. You mustn't blame yourself.

BROOKE. Sorry?

BELINDA. You're not going to cry. I'm not going to let you cry.

BROOKE. No, I've got something behind my lens.

FREDERICK. Yes, it's not Brooke's fault. You couldn't expect her to keep an eye on anyone.

DOTTY (*points at* SELSDON *without seeing him*). But he was standing right there in the stalls before we started! I saw him!

BROOKE. Who are we talking about now?

BELINDA. It's all right, my sweet. We know you can't see anything.

BROOKE. You mean *Selsdon*? I'm not *blind*. I can see *Selsdon*.

*They all turn and see him.*

BELINDA. Selsdon!

GARRY. Oh my God, he's here all the time!

LLOYD. Standing there like Hamlet's father.

FREDERICK. My word, Selsdon, you gave us a surprise. We thought you were . . . We thought you were — not there.

DOTTY. Where have you been, Selsdon?

BELINDA. Are you all right, Selsdon?

LLOYD. Speak to us!

SELSDON. Is it a party?

BELINDA. 'Is it a party?'!

SELSDON. Is it? How killing! I got it into my head there was going to be a rehearsal.

*He goes up on to the stage.*

I was having a little postprandial snooze at the back of the stalls so as to be ready for the rehearsal.

BELINDA. Isn't he lovely?

LLOYD. Much lovelier now we can see him.

SELSDON. So what are we celebrating?

BELINDA. 'What are we celebrating?'!

DOTTY. The old so-and-so.

LLOYD. We're celebrating seeing you, Selsdon.

SELSDON. Haven't missed the first night, have I?

BELINDA. Isn't he wonderful?

DOTTY. We'll let you know if you miss the first night, don't you worry. Or any other night.

LLOYD. We'll speak quite loudly and distinctly.

*Enter* TIM *from the wings. He waits anxiously to speak to* LLOYD.

SELSDON. Only I did miss a first night once, you know. It caused quite a flutter. This was in Liverpool, in 1934, and you remember what it was like then . . .

LLOYD. Vividly. Tim, you look strained and anxious. You're not trying to do too much, are you?

TIM. I can't find the gear. I've looked all through his dressing-room. I've looked all through the wardrobe.

LLOYD *indicates* SELSDON.

Oh.

SELSDON. Beer? In the wardrobe?

LLOYD. No, Selsdon. Tim, you need a break. Why don't you sit down quietly upstairs and do all the company's VAT?

TIM. I'll just do the bananas first.

*Exit* TIM *into the wings.*

BELINDA. He has been on his feet for forty-eight hours, Lloyd.

LLOYD (*calls*): Don't fall down, Tim. We may not be insured.

SELSDON. So what's next on the bill?

LLOYD. Well, Selsdon, I thought we might try a spot of rehearsal.

SELSDON. Oh, I won't, thank you.

LLOYD. You *won't*?

SELSDON. You all go ahead. I'll sit and watch you. This is the beer in the wardrobe, is it?

BELINDA. No, my sweet, he wants us to rehearse.

SELSDON. Yes, but I think we've got to rehearse, haven't we?

LLOYD. Rehearse, yes! Well done, Selsdon. I knew you'd think of something. Right, from Belinda and Freddie's entrance . . .

*Enter* POPPY *from the wings, alarmed.*

Oh my God, what's happened now?

POPPY. The police!

LLOYD. The *police*?

POPPY. They've found an old man. He was lying unconscious in a doorway just across the street.

LLOYD. Oh. Yes. Thank you.

POPPY. They say he's very dirty and rather smelly, and I thought, oh my God, because —

LLOYD. Thank you, Poppy.

POPPY. Because when you get close to Selsdon —

BELINDA. Poppy!

POPPY. No, I mean, if you stand anywhere near Selsdon you can't help noticing this very distinctive . . .

*She stops, sniffing.*

SELSDON. Why? He pongs a bit, does he?

BELINDA. No, no, no!

GARRY. Not you, love!

FREDERICK. Somebody else.

LLOYD. A dog, this is.

SELSDON. Oh.

GARRY (*softly*): Oh my God.

SELSDON (*to* POPPY, *putting an understanding arm round her*): A chap can take a hint, you know. All you've got to say is, 'There's this other chap I know who's got the most awful pong.' I'd get the point at once, if I were the young man in question.

*Exit* SELSDON *into the study.*

BELINDA. Oh, bless him!

DOTTY. Puts it on half the time, doesn't he.

LLOYD. Tell me, Poppy, love — how did you get a job like this, that requires tact and understanding? You're not somebody's girl-friend, are you?

POPPY *gives him a startled look.*

BELINDA. Don't worry, Poppy, my sweet. He truly did not hear.

*Enter* SELSDON *from the study.*

SELSDON. *Not* here?

LLOYD. Yes, yes, — there!

BELINDA. Sit down, my precious.

DOTTY. Go back to sleep.

LLOYD. You're not on for another twenty pages yet.

SELSDON. I think I might go back to sleep. I'm not on for another twenty pages yet.

*Exit* SELSDON *into the study. Exit* POPPY *into the wings.*

LLOYD. And on we go.

*He goes back down into the auditorium.*

Dotty in the kitchen, wildly roasting sardines. Freddie and Belinda waiting impatiently outside the front door. Garry and Brooke disappearing tremulously into the bedroom. Time sliding irrevocably into the past.

*Exeunt* DOTTY *into the service quarters,* GARRY *and* BROOKE *upstairs into the bedroom, and* FREDERICK *through the front door.*

BELINDA (*to* LLOYD, *with lowered voice*): Aren't they sweet?

LLOYD. What?

BELINDA. Garry and Dotty.

LLOYD. Garry and Dotty?

BELINDA. Sh!

LLOYD (*lowers his voice*): What? You mean they're . . .?

BELINDA. It's supposed to be a secret.

LLOYD. But she's old enough to be —

BELINDA. Sh!

LLOYD. *Garry*? And *Dotty*? Tramplemain and Mrs Clackett?

BELINDA. Didn't you know?

LLOYD (*in his ordinary voice*): I'm just God, Belinda, love. I'm just the one with the English degree, I don't know anything.

*Enter* GARRY *from the bedroom.*

GARRY. What's happening?

LLOYD. You tell me, Garry, honey.

*Exit* BELINDA *through the front door.*

GARRY. I mean, what are we waiting for?

*Enter* DOTTY *from the service quarters, inquiringly.*

LLOYD. I don't know what you're waiting for, Garry. Her sixteenth birthday?

GARRY. What?

LLOYD. Or maybe just the cue. Brooke!

*Exit* DOTTY *to the service quarters.*
*Enter* BROOKE *from the bedroom.*

LLOYD. 'You can't even get the door open.'

VICKI. You can't even get the door open.

LLOYD. Door closed, love.

GARRY *closes the door.*

VICKI. You can't even get the door open.

*Exeunt* ROGER *and* VICKI *into the bedroom.*
*Enter* PHILIP *through the front door.*

PHILIP. Yes, but this is Mrs Clackett's afternoon off.

*Enter* FLAVIA.

We've got the place entirely to ourselves.

PHILIP *brings in the flight bag and closes the door.*

FLAVIA. Look at it!

PHILIP. Do you like it?

FLAVIA. I can't believe it!

PHILIP. The perfect place for an assignation.

FLAVIA. Home.

PHILIP. Home.

FLAVIA. Our little secret hideaway.

PHILIP. The last place on earth anyone will look for us.

FLAVIA. It's rather funny, creeping in like this.

PHILIP. It's damned serious! If Inland Revenue find out we're in the country, even for one night, bang goes our claim to be resident abroad — bang goes most of this year's income. I feel like an illegal immigrant.

FLAVIA. I'll tell you what I feel like.

PHILIP. Champagne? (*Takes a bottle out of the box.*)

FLAVIA. I wonder if Mrs Clackett's aired the beds.

PHILIP. Darling!

FLAVIA. Well, why not? No children. No friends dropping in. We're absolutely on our own.

PHILIP. True. (*Picks up the bag and box and ushers FLAVIA towards the stairs.*) There is something to be said for being a tax exile.

FLAVIA. Leave those!

*He drops the bag and box and kisses her. She flees upstairs, laughing, and he after her.*

PHILIP. Sh!

FLAVIA. What?

PHILIP. Inland Revenue may hear us!

*They creep to the bedroom door.*
*Enter MRS CLACKETT from the service quarters carrying a fresh plate of sardines.*

MRS CLACKETT (*to herself*): What I did with that first lot of sardines I shall never know.

*She puts the sardines on the telephone table and sits on the sofa.*

PHILIP *and* FLAVIA (*looking down from the gallery*): Mrs Clackett!

MRS CLACKETT *jumps up.*

MRS CLACKETT. Oh, you give me a turn! My heart jumped right out of my boots!

PHILIP. So did mine!

FLAVIA. We thought you'd gone!

MRS CLACKETT. I thought you was in Spain!

PHILIP. We are! We are!

FLAVIA. You haven't seen us!

PHILIP. We're not here!

MRS CLACKETT. Oh, like that, is it? The income tax are after you?

FLAVIA. They would be, if they knew we were here.

MRS CLACKETT. All right, then, love. You're not here. I haven't seen you. Anybody asks for you, I don't know nothing. Off to bed, are you?

PHILIP. Oh . . .

FLAVIA. Well . . .

MRS CLACKETT. That's right. Nowhere like bed when they all get on top of you. You'll want your things, look. (*Indicates the bag and box.*)

PHILIP. Oh. Yes. Thanks.

*He comes downstairs, and picks up the bag and box.*

MRS CLACKETT (*to* FLAVIA): Oh, and that bed hasn't been aired, love.

FLAVIA. I'll get a hot water bottle.

*Exit* FLAVIA *into the mezzanine bathroom.*

MRS CLACKETT. I've put all your letters in the study, dear.

PHILIP. Letters? What letters? You forward all the mail, don't you?

MRS CLACKETT. Not the ones from the income tax, dear. I don't want to spoil your holidays.

PHILIP. Oh my God. Where are they?

MRS CLACKETT. I've put them all in the little pigeonhouse.

PHILIP. In the pigeonhouse?

MRS CLACKETT. In the little pigeonhouse in your desk, love.

*Exeunt* MRS CLACKETT *and* PHILIP *into the study.* PHILIP *is still holding the bag and box.*

*Only he remains on, and* DOTTY *remains in the doorway waiting for him.*

*Enter* ROGER *from the bedroom, still dressed, tying his tie.*

ROGER. Yes, but I could hear voices!

*Enter* VICKI *from the bedroom in her underwear.*

VICKI. Voices? What sort of voices?

LLOYD. Hold it. Freddie, what's the trouble?

FREDERICK. Lloyd, you know how stupid I am about moves. Sorry, Garry — sorry, Brooke — it's just my usual dimness. (*To* Lloyd:) But why do I take the things off into the study? Wouldn't it be more natural if I left them on?

LLOYD. No.

FREDERICK. I just thought it might be somehow more logical.

LLOYD. No.

FREDERICK. Lloyd, I know it's a bit late in the day to go into all this . . .

LLOYD. No, Freddie, we've got several more minutes left before we open.

*Enter* BELINDA *from the mezzanine bathroom, to wait patiently.*

FREDERICK. Thank you, Lloyd. As long as we're not too pushed. But I've never understood why he carries an overnight bag and a box of groceries into the study to look at his mail.

GARRY. Because they have to be out of the way for my next scene!

FREDERICK. I see that.

BELINDA. And Freddie, my sweet, Selsdon needs them in the

study for *his* scene.

FREDERICK. I see that . . .

LLOYD. Selsdon — where is he? Is he there?

BELINDA (*calls, urgently*): Selsdon!

DOTTY (*likewise*): Selsdon!

GARRY (*likewise*): Selsdon!

*Enter* SELSDON *through the window in haste.*

SELSDON. Am I on?

OMNES. No, no, no.

SELSDON. I thought I heard my voice.

LLOYD. No, no, no. Back to sleep, Selsdon. Another ten pages yet.

SELSDON. Oh.

*Exit* SELSDON *through the window.*

FREDERICK. All right, I see all that.

LLOYD (*faintly*): Oh, no!

FREDERICK. I just don't know why I take them.

LLOYD *comes up on stage.*

LLOYD. Freddie, love, why does anyone do anything? Why does that other idiot walk out through the front door holding two plates of sardines? (*To* GARRY:) I mean, I'm not getting at you, love.

GARRY. Of course not, love. (*To* FREDERICK:) I mean, why *do* I? (*To* LLOYD:) I mean, Jesus, when you come to think about it, why *do* I?

LLOYD. Who knows?

GARRY. Who knows, you see, Freddie, love?

LLOYD (*to* FREDERICK): The wellsprings of human action are deep and cloudy. Maybe something happened to you as a very small child which made you frightened to let go of groceries.

BELINDA. Or it could be genetic.

GARRY. Yes, or it could be, you know.

LLOYD. It could well be.

FREDERICK. Of course. Thank you. I understand all that. But . . .

LLOYD. Freddie, love, I'm telling you — I don't know. I don't think the author knows. I don't know why the author came into this industry in the first place. I don't know why any of us came into it.

FREDERICK. All the same, if you could just give me a reason I could keep in my mind . . .

LLOYD. All right, I'll give you a reason. You carry those groceries into the study, Freddie, honey, because it's just slightly after midnight, and we're not going to be finished before we open tomorrow night. Correction — before we open *tonight.*

FREDERICK *nods, and exits into the study.* DOTTY *silently follows him.* GARRY *and* BROOKE *go silently back into the bedroom.* LLOYD *returns to the stalls.*

And on we go. From after Freddie's exit, *with* the groceries.

BELINDA (*keeping her voice down*): Lloyd, sweetheart, his wife left him this morning.

LLOYD. Oh. Freddie!

*Enter* FREDERICK *from the study.*

I think the point is that you've had a great fright when she mentions income tax, and you feel very insecure and exposed, and you want something familiar to hold on to.

FREDERICK (*with humble gratitude*): Thank you, Lloyd.

*Exit* FREDERICK *into the study.*

BELINDA (*to* LLOYD): Bless you, my sweet.

LLOYD. And on we merrily go.

*Exit* BELINDA *into the mezzanine bathroom.*

'Yes, but I could hear voices . . .'

*Enter* ROGER *from the bedroom, still dressed, tying his tie.*

ROGER. Yes, but I could hear voices!

*Enter* VICKI *from the bedroom in her underwear.*

VICKI. Voices? What sort of voices?

ROGER. People's voices.

VICKI. But there's no one here.

ROGER. Darling, I saw the door-handle move! It could be someone from the office, checking up.

VICKI. I still don't see why you've got to put your tie on to look.

ROGER. Mrs Clockett.

VICKI. Mrs Clockett?

ROGER. She's been in the family for generations.

VICKI (*looks over the bannisters*): Oh, look, she's opened our sardines.

*She moves to go downstairs.* ROGER *grabs her.*

ROGER. Come back!

VICKI. What?

ROGER. I'll fetch them! You can't go downstairs like that.

VICKI. Why not?

ROGER. Mrs Crackett.

VICKI. Mrs Crackett?

ROGER. She's irreplaceable.

*Enter* MRS CLACKETT *from the study. She is carrying the first plate of sardines.*

MRS CLACKETT (*to herself*): Sardines here. Sardines there. It's like a Sunday school outing.

ROGER *pushes* VICKI *through the first available door, which happens to be the linen cupboard.*

Oh, you're still poking around, are you?

ROGER. Yes, still poking — well, still around.

MRS CLACKETT. In the airing cupboard, were you?

ROGER. No, no. (*The linen cupboard door begins to open. He slams it shut.*) Well, just checking the sheets and pillow-cases. Going through the inventory.

*He starts downstairs.*

Mrs Blackett . . .

MRS CLACKETT. Clackett, dear, Clackett.

*She puts down the sardines beside the other sardines.*

ROGER. Mrs Clackett. Is there anyone else in the house, Mrs Clackett?

MRS CLACKETT. I haven't seen no one, dear.

ROGER. I thought I heard voices.

MRS CLACKETT. Voices? There's no voices here, love.

ROGER. I must have imagined it.

PHILIP (*off*): Oh my God!

ROGER, *with his back to her, picks up both plates of sardines.*

ROGER. I beg your pardon?

MRS CLACKETT (*mimics* PHILIP): Oh my God!

ROGER. Why, what is it?

MRS CLACKETT. Oh my God, the study door's open.

*She crosses and closes it.* ROGER *looks out of the window.*

ROGER. There's another car outside! That's not Mr Hackham's, is it? Or Mr Dudley's?

*Exit* ROGER *through the front door, holding both plates of sardines. Enter* FLAVIA *from the mezzanine bathroom, carrying a hot water bottle. She sees the linen cupboard door swinging open as she passes, pushes it shut, and turns the key.*

FLAVIA. Nothing but flapping doors in this house.

*Exit* FLAVIA *into the bedroom.*
*Enter from the study* PHILIP, *holding a tax demand and its envelope.*

PHILIP. '. . . final notice . . . steps will be taken . . . distraint . . . proceedings in court . . .'

MRS CLACKETT. Oh yes, and that reminds me, a gentleman come about the house.

PHILIP. Don't tell me. I'm not here.

MRS CLACKETT. He says he's got a lady quite aroused.

PHILIP. Leave everything to Squire, Squire, Hackham and Dudley.

MRS CLACKETT. All right, love. I'll let them go all over, shall I?

PHILIP. Let them do anything. Just so long as you don't tell anyone we're here.

MRS CLACKETT. So I'll just sit down and turn on the . . . sardines, I've forgotten the sardines! I don't know — if it wasn't fixed to my shoulders I'd forget what day it was.

*Exit* MRS CLACKETT *to the service quarters.*

PHILIP. I didn't get this! I'm not here. I'm in Spain. But if I didn't get it I didn't open it.

*Enter* FLAVIA *from the bedroom. She is holding the dress that* VICKI *arrived in.*

FLAVIA. Darling, I never had a dress like this, did I?

PHILIP (*abstracted*): Didn't you?

FLAVIA. I shouldn't buy anything as tarty as this . . . Oh, it's not something you gave me, is it?

PHILIP. I should never have touched it.

FLAVIA. No, it's lovely.

PHILIP. Stick it down. Put it back. Never saw it.

*Exit* PHILIP *into study.*

FLAVIA. Well, I'll put it in the attic, with all the other things you gave me that are too precious to wear.

*Exit* FLAVIA *along the upstairs corridor.*
*Enter* ROGER *through the front door, still carrying both plates of sardines.*

ROGER. All right, all right . . . Now the study door's open again! What's going on?

*He puts the sardines down — one plate on the telephone table, where it was before, one near the front door — and goes towards the study, but stops at the sound of urgent knocking overhead.*

Knocking! (*Knocking.*) Upstairs!

*Runs upstairs. Knocking.*

Oh my God, there's something in the airing cupboard!

*Unlocks it and opens it. Enter* VICKI.

Oh, it's you.

VICKI. Of course it's me! You put me in here! In the dark! With all black sheets and things!

ROGER. But, darling, why did you lock the door?

VICKI. Why did *I* lock the door? Why did *you* lock the door!

ROGER. *I* didn't lock the door!

VICKI. *Someone* locked the door!

ROGER. Anyway, we can't stand here like this.

VICKI. Like what?

ROGER. In your underwear.

VICKI. OK, I'll take it off.

ROGER. In here, in here!

*Ushers her into the bedroom.*

*Only she remains on, blinking anxiously, and peering about the floor.* GARRY *waits for her, holding the bedroom door open.*

> *Enter* PHILIP *from the study, holding the tax demand, the envelope, and a tube of glue.*

PHILIP. Darling, this glue. It's not that special quick-drying sort, is it, that you can never get unstuck . . .?

LLOYD. Hold it.

PHILIP. Oh, Mrs Clackett's made us some sardines.

LLOYD. Hold it. We have a problem.

FREDERICK (*to* BROOKE): Oh, bad luck! Which one is it this time?

BROOKE. Left.

GARRY (*calls to people off*): It's the left one, everybody!

OMNES (*off*): Left one! (*Enter* DOTTY, BELINDA, *and* POPPY.)

FREDERICK. It could be anywhere.

GARRY (*looks over the edge of the gallery*): It could have gone over the thing and fallen down, you know — and then bounced somewhere else again.

BROOKE *comes downstairs. They all search hopelessly.*

POPPY. Where did you last see it?

BELINDA. She *didn't* see it, poor sweet! It was in her eye!

GARRY (*comes downstairs*): It was probably on 'Why did *I* lock the door?' I say, 'But, darling, why did you lock the door?' She says, 'Why did *I* lock the door?' and she opens her eyes very sort of, you know. Don't you, my sweet? Actually there are several places where you open your eyes very sort of. I always feel I ought to rush forward and.

*He rushes forward, hands held out.*

DOTTY. Mind where you put your feet, my love.

FREDERICK. Yes, everyone look under their feet.

GARRY. No one move their feet.

BELINDA. Everyone put their feet back exactly where they were.

FREDERICK. Pick your feet up one by one.

*They all trample about, looking under their feet, except BROOKE, who crouches with her good eye at floor level. LLOYD comes up on stage.*

LLOYD. Brooke, love, is this going to happen during a performance? We don't want the audience to miss their last buses and trains.

BELINDA. She'll just carry on. Won't you, my love?

FREDERICK. But can she see anything without them?

LLOYD. Can she hear anything without them?

BROOKE (*suddenly realising that she is being addressed*): Sorry?

*She straightens up sharply. Her head comes in abrupt contact with POPPY's face.*

POPPY. Ugh!

BROOKE. Oh. Sorry.

BROOKE *jumps up to see what damage she has done to POPPY, and steps backward on to GARRY's hand.*

GARRY. Ugh!

BROOKE. Sorry?

*DOTTY hurries to his aid.*

DOTTY. Oh my poor darling! (*To* BROOKE:) You stood on his hand!

*FREDERICK claps a handkerchief to his nose.*

BELINDA. Oh, look at Freddie, the poor love!

FREDERICK (*looks into the handkerchief*): Excuse me.

*Exit FREDERICK hurriedly.*

LLOYD. What's the matter with *him*?

BELINDA. He's just got a little nosebleed, my sweet.

LLOYD. A nosebleed? No one touched him!

BELINDA. No, he's got a thing about violence. It always makes his nose bleed.

LLOYD. But where's he gone?

BELINDA. Well, he's got a thing about blood.

BROOKE. Sorry. Sorry. (*To* LLOYD:) I thought you said something to me.

LLOYD. Yes.

*He picks up a vase and hands it to her.*

Just go and hit the box-office manager with this, and you'll have finished off live theatre in Weston-super-Mare.

BROOKE. Anyway, I've found it.

BELINDA. She's found it!

DOTTY. Where was it, love?

BROOKE. In my eye.

GARRY. In her eye!

BELINDA (*hugs her*): Well done, my sweet.

LLOYD. Not in your left eye?

BROOKE. It had gone round the side.

BELINDA. I knew it hadn't gone far. Are you all right, Poppy, my sweet?

POPPY. I think so.

LLOYD. All right, clear the stage. Walking wounded carry the stretcher cases.

LLOYD *returns to the stalls*, DOTTY *to the service quarters*, POPPY *to the wings*. BELINDA, GARRY *and* BROOKE *go upstairs. Enter* FREDERICK.

BELINDA. Are you all right, Freddie, my pet?

FREDERICK. Fine. It's just that I've got this thing about, well, I won't say the word.

BELINDA. We all understand, my precious.

LLOYD. Right, then. On we bloodily stagger. Oh, sorry, Freddie. Let me rephrase that. On we blindly stumble. Brooke, I withdraw that.

*Exit* BELINDA *along upstairs corridor,* FREDERICK *into study.*

From your exit, anyway. 'OK, I'll take it off. — In here, in here.' Where's Selsdon?

GARRY. Selsdon!

LLOYD. Selsdon!

*Enter* SELSDON *through the front door.*

SELSDON. I think she might have dropped it out here somewhere.

LLOYD. Good. Keep looking. Only another five pages, Selsdon.

*Exit* SELSDON *through the front door.*

'Anyway, we can't stand here like this. — Like what? — In your underwear. — OK, I'll take it off . . .'

ROGER. In here, in here!

> *Ushers her into the bedroom.*
> *Enter* PHILIP *from the study, holding the tax demand, the envelope, and a tube of glue.*

PHILIP. Darling, this glue. It's not that special quick-drying sort, is it, that you can never get unstuck . . . ? Oh, Mrs Clackett's made us some sardines.

> *Exit* PHILIP *into the study with the tax demand, envelope, glue and one of the plates of sardines from the telephone table.*
> *Enter* ROGER *from the bedroom, holding the hot water bottle. He looks up and down the landing.*
> *Enter* VICKI *from the bedroom.*

VICKI. Now what?

ROGER. A hot water bottle! *I* didn't put it there!

VICKI. *I* didn't put it there.

ROGER. Someone in the bathroom, filling hot water bottles.

> *Exit* ROGER *into the mezzanine bathroom.*

VICKI (*anxious*): You don't think there's something creepy going on?

*Exit* VICKI *into the mezzanine bathroom.*
*Enter* FLAVIA *along the upstairs corridor.*

FLAVIA. Darling, are you coming to bed or aren't you?

*Exit* FLAVIA *into the bedroom.*
*Enter* ROGER *and* VICKI *from the mezzanine bathroom.*

ROGER. What did you say?

VICKI. I didn't say anything.

ROGER. I mean, first the door handle. Now the hot water
bottle . . .

VICKI. I can feel goose-pimples all over.

ROGER. Yes, quick, get something round you.

VICKI. Get the covers over our heads.

ROGER *is about to open the bedroom door.*

ROGER. Just a moment. What did I do with those sardines?

*He goes downstairs.* VICKI *makes to follow.*

You — wait here.

VICKI (*uneasy*): You hear all sorts of funny things about
these old houses.

ROGER. Yes, but this one has been extensively modernised
throughout. I can't see how anything creepy would
survive oil-fired central heating and . . .

VICKI. What? What is it?

*ROGER stares at the telephone table in silence.*
*The bedroom door opens, and* FLAVIA *puts* VICKI's
*flight bag on the table outside without looking round.*
*The door closes again.*

VICKI. What's happening?

ROGER. The sardines. They've gone.

VICKI. Perhaps there is something funny going on. I'm
going to get into bed and put my head under the . . .

*She freezes at the sight of the flight bag.*

ROGER. I put them there. Or was it *there*?

VICKI. Bag . . .

*VICKI runs down the stairs to* ROGER, *who is directly underneath the gallery.*

ROGER. I suppose Mrs Sprockett must have taken them away again . . . What? What is it?

VICKI. Bag!

ROGER. Bag?

VICKI. Bag! Bag!

*Enter* FLAVIA *from the bedroom with the box of files. She picks up the flight bag as well, and takes them both off along the upstairs corridor. As she does so,* VICKI *drags* ROGER *back upstairs.*

ROGER. What do you mean, bag, bag?

VICKI. Bag! Bag! Bag!

ROGER. What bag?

*VICKI sees the empty table outside the bedroom door.*

VICKI. No bag!

ROGER. No bag?

VICKI. Your bag! Suddenly! Here! Now — gone!

ROGER. It's in the bedroom. I put it in the bedroom.

*Exit* ROGER *into the bedroom.*

VICKI. Don't go in there!

*Enter* ROGER *from the bedroom.*

ROGER. The box!

VICKI. The box?

ROGER. They've both gone!

VICKI. Oh! My files!

ROGER. What on earth's happening? Where's Mrs Spratchett?

*He starts downstairs.* VICKI *follows him.*

You wait in the bedroom.

VICKI. No! No! No!

*She runs downstairs.*

ROGER. Well, get dressed, then!

VICKI. I'm not going in there!

ROGER. I'll fetch your dress out here.

*Exit ROGER into the bedroom.*
*Enter ROGER from the bedroom.*

Your dress has gone.

VICKI. Oh!

*ROGER goes downstairs.*

ROGER. Don't panic! Don't panic! There's some perfectly
rational explanation for all this. I'll fetch Mrs Splotchett
and she'll tell us what's happening. You wait here . . .
You can't stand here looking like that . . . You wait
in the study . . . Study, study, study!

*Exit ROGER into the service quarters.*
*VICKI opens the study door. There is a roar of*
*exasperation from PHILIP, off. She turns and flees.*

VICKI. Roger! There's something in there! Where are you?

*There is another cry from PHILIP, off.*
*Exit VICKI blindly through the front door.*
*Enter PHILIP from the study. He is holding the tax*
*demand in his right hand, and one of the plates of*
*sardines in his left.*

PHILIP. Darling, I know this is going to sound silly, but . . .

*He struggles to get the tax demand unstuck from his*
*fingers, encumbered by the plate of sardines.*
*Enter FLAVIA along the upstairs corridor, carrying*
*various pieces of bric-à-brac.*

FLAVIA. Darling, if we're not going to bed I'm going to
clear out the attic.

PHILIP. Darling, I can't come to bed! I'm glued to a tax demand!

FLAVIA. Darling, why don't you put the sardines down?

> PHILIP *puts the plate of sardines down on the table. But when he takes his hand away the sardines come with it.*

PHILIP. Darling, I'm stuck to the sardines!

FLAVIA. Darling, don't play the fool. Get that bottle marked poison in the downstairs loo. That eats through anything.

> *Exit* FLAVIA *along the upstairs corridor.*

PHILIP (*flaps the tax demand*): I've heard of people getting stuck with a *problem,* but this is ridiculous.

> *Exit* PHILIP *into the downstairs bathroom.*

*Pause.*

LLOYD. Selsdon . . .? You're on, Selsdon. We're there. The moment's arrived . . .

BELINDA (*off*): It's all right, love. He's coming, he's coming . . .

LLOYD. But there should be an arm coming through that window even before Freddie's off!

> *A pane of glass shatters in the mullioned window, and an arm comes through and releases the catch.*

LLOYD. Ah. Here it comes. An arm clothed in white samite, mystic, wonderful. And just too late to catch the bloody sword.

> *The window opens, and through it appears an elderly* BURGLAR. *He has great character, but is in need of extensive repair and modernisation.*

> BURGLAR. No bars, no burglar alarm. They ought to be prosecuted for incitement.

> *He climbs in.*

LLOYD. All right, Selsdon, hold it. Let's take it again.

BURGLAR. No, but sometimes it makes me want to
sit down and weep. When I think I used to do banks!
When I remember I used to do bullion vaults! What am
I doing now? — I'm breaking into paper bags!

LLOYD. Hold it, Selsdon. Hold it!

*Pours himself a drink.*

LLOYD. *Hold it!*

*Enter POPPY from the wings.*

BURGLAR. I know they're all in Spain, 'cause the old
turkey in the kitchen told me so . . .

POPPY. Lloyd wants you to hold it.

*Enter BELINDA.*

BURGLAR. And I know *she's* out, cause I've just seen her
come out of the front door in her swimming costume . . .

BELINDA. Stop, Selsdon, my love! Wait, my precious!

SELSDON *stops, restrained at last by* BELINDA's *hand on
his arm.*

LLOYD. My God, it's like Myra Hess playing on through the
air-raids.

SELSDON. Stop?

POPPY. Stop.

BELINDA. Stop.

LLOYD. Thank you, Belinda. Thank you, Poppy.

*Exeunt BELINDA and POPPY.*

Selsdon . . .

SELSDON. I met Myra Hess once.

LLOYD. I think he can hear better than I can.

SELSDON. I beg your pardon?

LLOYD. From your entrance, please, Selsdon.

SELSDON. Well, it was during the war, at a charity show in
Sunderland . . .

LLOYD. Thank you! Poppy!

SELSDON. Oh, not for me. It stops me sleeping.

*Enter* POPPY *from the wings.*

LLOYD. Put the glass back, will you?

SELSDON. Come on again?

LLOYD. Right. Only, Selsdon . . .

SELSDON. Yes?

LLOYD. A little sooner, Selsdon. A shade earlier. Like *yesterday.*
Freddie!

*Enter* FREDERICK *from the downstairs bathroom.*

(*To* SELSDON:) Start moving as soon as Freddie opens the
door. (*To* FREDERICK:) What's the line?

FREDERICK. 'I've heard of people getting stuck with a *problem,*
but this is ridiculous.'

LLOYD. Start moving as soon as you hear the line, 'I've heard
of people getting *stuck* with a problem . . .'

FREDERICK. '*Stuck* with a problem'?

LLOYD. '*Stuck* with a problem, but this is ridiculous.' And I
want your arm through that window. Right?

SELSDON. Say no more. May I make just one suggestion, though?

LLOYD. What is it, Selsdon?

SELSDON. Should I perhaps come on a little earlier?

LLOYD. Selsdon . . .

SELSDON. Only there does seem to be something of a hiatus
between Freddie's exit and my entrance.

LLOYD. No, Selsdon. Listen. Don't worry. I've got it.

SELSDON. Yes?

LLOYD. How about coming on a little earlier?

SELSDON. We're obviously thinking along the same lines.

*Exit* SELSDON *through the window.*

Enter FREDERICK *from the downstairs bathroom.*

LLOYD. Am I putting him on or is he putting me on? Right,
Freddie, from your exit.

PHILIP (*flaps the tax demand*): I've heard of people getting
*stuck* with a problem, but this is ridiculous.

*Exit* PHILIP *into downstairs bathroom.*
*Enter* BURGLAR *as before, but on time.*

BURGLAR. No bars, no burglar alarms. They ought to be
prosecuted for incitement.

*He climbs in.*

BURGLAR. No, but sometimes it makes me want to sit
down and weep. When I think I used to do banks! When
I remember I used to do bullion vaults! What am I
doing now? — I'm breaking into paper bags!

*Pours himself a drink.*

I know they're all in Spain, cause the old turkey in the
kitchen told me so. And I know *she's* out, 'cause I've
just seen her come out the front door in her swimming
costume . . . Where is the front door . . . ?

*Peers shortsightedly, then opens the front door ready
for his departure.*

Right, get the van loaded. No rush. I've only got all
flaming afternoon! What are they offering? (*Peers at the
television.*) One microwave oven.

*Unplugs it and puts it on the sofa.*

What? Fifty quid? Hardly worth lifting it.

*Picks up his drink and inspects the paintings and
ornaments.*

Junk . . . Junk . . . If you insist . . .

*Pockets some small item.*

Where's his desk? No, they all say the same thing — it's
hard to adjust to retirement.

*Exit* BURGLAR *into the study, holding his drink.*

*Enter* ROGER *from the service quarters, followed by* MRS CLACKETT, *who is holding another plate of sardines.*

ROGER. . . . And the prospective tenant naturally wishes to know if there is any previous history of paranormal phenomena.

MRS CLACKETT. Oh, yes, dear, it's all nice and paranormal.

ROGER. I mean, has anything ever dematerialised before? Has anything ever flown about?

MRS CLACKETT *puts the sardines down on the telephone table, moves the television set back, plugs it in, and closes the front door.*

MRS CLACKETT. Flown about? No, the things move themselves on their own two feet, just like they do in any house.

ROGER. I'll tell the prospective tenant. She is inspecting the study.

*He opens the study door and then closes it again.*

There's a man in there!

MRS CLACKETT. No, no, there's no one in the house, love.

ROGER (*opens the study door*): Look! Look! He's . . . *searching* for something.

MRS CLACKETT (*glances briefly*): I can't see no one.

ROGER. You can't see him? But this is extraordinary! And where is my prospective tenant? I left her in there! She's gone! My prospective tenant has disappeared!

*He closes the study door, and looks round the living room. He sees the sardines on the telephone table.*

Oh my God.

MRS CLACKETT. Now what?

ROGER. There!

MRS CLACKETT. Where?

ROGER. The sardines!

MRS CLACKETT. Oh, the sardines.

ROGER. You can see the sardines, can you?

MRS CLACKETT. I can see the sardines.

> ROGER *touches them cautiously, then picks up the plate.*

I can see the way they're going, too.

ROGER. I'm not letting these sardines out of my hand. But where is my prospective tenant?

> *He goes upstairs, holding the sardines.*

MRS CLACKETT. I can see I'm going to be opening sardines all night, in and out of here like the cuckoo on a clock.

> *Exit MRS CLACKETT into the service quarters.*

ROGER. Vicki! Vicki!

> *Exit ROGER into the mezzanine bathroom.*
> *Enter BURGLAR from the study, carrying an armful of silver cups, etc.*

BURGLAR. he said, 'Charles,' he said, 'You're seventy years old. It's time to hang up the sawn-off shotgun. It's time to let a younger man take over the ammonia bottle.'

> *Dumps the silverware on the sofa, and exit into study.*
> *Enter ROGER from mezzanine bathroom.*

ROGER. Where's she gone? She hasn't gone back in the bedroom?

> *Exit ROGER into the bedroom.*
> *Enter BURGLAR from the study, carrying PHILIP's box and bag. He empties the contents of the box out behind the sofa, and loads the silverware into the box.*

BURGLAR. I said, 'I may be seventy, but I've still got all my wits about me.' He didn't have any answer to that.

> *Enter ROGER from the bedroom, still holding the sardines.*

ROGER (*calls*): Vicki! Vicki!

> *Exit* ROGER *into the linen cupboard.*

BURGLAR. Or if he did, *I* didn't hear it.

> *Exit* BURGLAR *into study, not having seen or heard* ROGER.
> *Enter* PHILIP *from the downstairs bathroom. His right hand is still stuck to the tax demand, his left to the plate of sardines.*

PHILIP. Darling, this stuff that eats through anything. It doesn't eat through glue . . . It just eats through *trousers!* Darling, if it eats through trousers, you don't think it goes on and eats through . . . Listen, darling, I think I'd better get these trousers off! (*He begins to do so, as best he can.*) Darling, quick, this is an emergency! Have we got any stuff that stops the stuff that stops the stuff? I mean, if it eats through absolutely anything . . . Darling, I think I can feel it! I think it's eating through . . absolutely everything!

> *Enter* ROGER *from the linen cupboard, still holding the sardines.*

ROGER. There's something evil in this house.

> PHILIP *pulls up his trousers.*

PHILIP (*aside*): The Inland Revenue!

ROGER (*frightened*): He's back!

PHILIP. No!

ROGER. No?

PHILIP. I'm not here.

ROGER. Oh my God.

PHILIP. I'm abroad.

ROGER. He's walking abroad.

PHILIP. I must go.

ROGER. Stay!

PHILIP. I'm not staying.

ROGER. Speak!

PHILIP. Only in the presence of my lawyer.

ROGER. Only in the . . . ? Hold on. Hold on. You're just
an intruder, an ordinary intruder!

PHILIP. Well, nice to meet you.

*Waves goodbye with his right hand, then sees the tax
demand on it, and hurriedly puts it away behind his back.*

I mean, have a sardine.

*Offers the sardines on his left hand. His trousers,
unsupported, fall down.*

ROGER. No, you're not! You're some kind of sex criminal!
You've done something to Vicki! I'm going to come
downstairs and sort you out!

ROGER *comes downstairs and dials 999.*

PHILIP. Oh, you've got some sardines. Well, if there's
nothing I can offer you . . .

ROGER (*into the phone*): Police!

PHILIP. . . . I think I'll be running along.

*Runs, his trousers still round his ankles. Exit through
front door.*

ROGER. Come back . . .! (*Into the phone*:) Hello — police?
Someone has broken into my house! Or rather someone
has broken into someone's house . . . Yes, a sex criminal!
And a young woman is missing!

*Enter VICKI through the window.*

VICKI. It's in the garden now, and it's a man!

ROGER (*into the phone*): Sorry — the young woman has
reappeared. (*Hand over phone*:) Are you all right?

VICKI. No, he almost saw me!

ROGER (*into the phone*): He almost saw her . . . No, but
he's a burglar as well! He's taken our things!

VICKI (*finds* PHILIP's *bag and box*): The things are here.

ROGER (*into the phone*): The things have come back. So we're just missing a plate of sardines.

VICKI (*finds the sardines left near the front door by* ROGER): Here are the sardines.

ROGER (*into the phone*): And we've found the sardines.

VICKI. This is the police? You want the police here — in my underwear?

ROGER (*into the phone*): So what am I saying? I'm saying, Let's say no more about it. (*Puts the phone down.*) I thought something terrible had happened to you!

VICKI. It has! I know him!

ROGER. You know him?

VICKI. He's dealt with by our office!

ROGER. He's just an ordinary sex criminal.

VICKI. Yes, but he mustn't see me like this! You have to keep up certain standards if you work for Inland Revenue!

ROGER. Well, put something on!

VICKI. I haven't got anything!

ROGER. There must be something in the bathroom!

*He picks up the box and bag and leads the way upstairs towards the mezzanine bathroom.*

Bring the sardines!

*Exeunt* ROGER *and* VICKI *into the mezzanine bathroom.*
*Enter the* BURGLAR *from the study, carrying a tape-recorder.*

BURGLAR. 'What?' I said. 'When have I ever needed to run off in the middle of a job to have a Jimmy Riddle?'

*Puts the tape-recorder down by the front door.*

BURGLAR. 'Except when some stupid berk goes and starts talking about it . . . ?' Oh, my Gawd! Where is it?

*Enter* ROGER *from the mezzanine bathroom, carrying the box and bag.*

ROGER. Just stay in there.

*Enter* VICKI *from the mezzanine bathroom, holding up a very short off-the-shoulder white nightdress.*

And don't come out till you've got dressed.

*Exit* ROGER *into the bedroom.*

VICKI. But I can't go around in front of our taxpayers wearing *this*!

*Exit* VICKI *into the bedroom.*

BURGLAR. I knew I shouldn't have brought the subject up.

*Exit* BURGLAR *into the open door of the mezzanine bathroom.*
*Enter* PHILIP *through the front door.*

PHILIP. Darling! Help! Where are you?

*Enter* VICKI *from the bedroom, holding the nightdress, followed by* ROGER.
*Exit* PHILIP *hurriedly into the downstairs bathroom.*

ROGER. Just put it on! It's a start, at any rate! I'll find a bottom – I'll find a top – I'll find something.

*Exit* ROGER *into the bedroom.*
*Exit* VICKI *into the mezzanine bathroom.*
*Enter* VICKI *from the mezzanine bathroom.*

VICKI. Someone in there! It's *him*!

*Exit* VICKI *hurriedly into the downstairs bathroom.*
*Enter* FLAVIA *along the upstairs corridor, carrying an old biscuit tin.*

FLAVIA. Oh, darling, I'm finding such lovely things!

VICKI *screams, off.*

Do you remember this old biscuit tin . . .

*Enter* VICKI *from the downstairs bathroom. She stops at the sight of* FLAVIA.

. . . you gave me on the very first anniversary of our . . .?
Who are you?

VICKI. Oh my God, it's his wife and dependents!

*She puts her hands over her face.*
*Enter PHILIP from the downstairs bathroom, still with
his hands encumbered, holding the nightdress now as
well, and keeping his trousers up with his elbows.*

PHILIP. I've taken your dress off you!

*FLAVIA gasps. PHILIP looks up at the gallery and sees
her.*

(*To* FLAVIA:) Where have you been? I've been going
mad! Look at the state I'm in!

*He holds up his hands to show FLAVIA the state he
is in, and his trousers fall down.*
*The biscuit tin slips from FLAVIA's horrified hands,
and crashes on the floor of the living room below.*
*PHILIP hurries towards the stairs, trousers around his
ankles, hands extended in supplication.*
*VICKI flees before him and takes refuge in the linen
cupboard.*

PHILIP. Darling, I was just trying to explain to her about
Inland Revenue being after us, and my fingers got stuck!

*Exit FLAVIA, with a cry of pain, along the upstairs
corridor.*
*Enter ROGER from the bedroom, directly in PHILIP's
path. PHILIP holds up the nightdress in front of his face.*

ROGER. Don't keep waving that thing in my face! I'm
*trying* to find something! I'll look in the other rooms.

*Exit ROGER along upstairs corridor.*
*PHILIP turns to go back downstairs. The mezzanine
lavatory flushes. He stops.*
*Enter the BURGLAR from the mezzanine bathroom,
holding two gold taps.*

BURGLAR. One pair gold taps, anyway . . .

*He stops at the sight of* PHILIP.

Oh, my Gawd!

PHILIP. Who are you?

BURGLAR. Me? Fixing the taps.

PHILIP. Tax? Income tax?

BURGLAR. That's right, governor. In come new taps —
out go the old taps.

*Exit* BURGLAR *into the mezzanine bathroom.*

PHILIP. Tax-inspectors everywhere!

ROGER (*off*): Oh my God!

PHILIP. The other one!

*Exit* PHILIP *into the bedroom, holding the nightdress
in front of his face.*
*Enter* ROGER *along the upstairs corridor.*

ROGER. Tin boxes flying about! There *is* something funny
going on here! Are you dressed yet?

*Exit* ROGER *into mezzanine bathroom.*
*Enter* PHILIP *from the bedroom, trying to pull the
nightdress off his head.*

PHILIP. Darling! I've got the dress stuck to my head now!

*Enter* ROGER *from the mezzanine bathroom.*
*Exit* PHILIP *into the bedroom.*

ROGER. A man!

*Enter the* BURGLAR *from the mezzanine bathroom.*

BURGLAR. Just doing the taps, governor.

ROGER.  Attacks? Not attacks on women.

BURGLAR. Try anything, governor, but I'll do the taps
on the bath first.

*Exit* BURGLAR *into the mezzanine bathroom.*

ROGER. Sex criminals everywhere! Where is Vicki?
Vicki . . .?

*Exit* ROGER *into the downstairs bathroom.*
*Enter* BURGLAR *from the mezzanine bathroom, heading for the front door.*

BURGLAR. People everywhere! I'm off. A tax on women? I don't know, they'll put a tax on anything these days.

*Enter* ROGER *from the downstairs bathroom. The* BURGLAR *makes a U-turn and heads back towards the mezzanine bathroom.*

ROGER. If I can't find her, you're going to be in trouble, you see.

BURGLAR. W.C.? I'll fix it.

*Exit* BURGLAR *into the mezzanine bathroom.*

ROGER. Vicki . . .?

*Exit* ROGER *through the front door.*
*Enter* PHILIP *from the bedroom. The nightdress is still on his head, but is now arranged like a burnous, and he is wrapped in a white bedsheet.*
*Enter* VICKI *from the linen cupboard, enrobed from head to foot in a black bedsheet. They close the doors behind them. The sound makes them see each other and start back.*
*Enter* ROGER *through the front door.*

ROGER. Sheikh! I thought you were coming at four?
And this is your charming wife? So you want to see over the house now, do you, Sheikh? Right. Well. Since you're upstairs already . . .

ROGER *goes upstairs.*
*Enter* FLAVIA *along the upstairs corridor, carrying a vase.*

FLAVIA. Him and his floozie! I'll break this over their heads!

ROGER. . . . let's start downstairs.

ROGER, PHILIP *and* VICKI *go downstairs.*

FLAVIA. Who are you? Who are these creatures?

ROGER (*to* PHILIP *and* VICKI): I'm sorry about this. I
   don't know who she is. No connection with the house,
   I assure you.

   *Enter* MRS CLACKETT *from the service quarters, with
   another plate of sardines.* ROGER *advances to introduce
   her.*

   Whereas this good lady with the sardines, on the other
   hand . . .

MRS CLACKETT. No other hands, thank you, not in my
   sardines, 'cause this time I'm eating them.

ROGER. . . . is fully occupied with her sardines, so perhaps
   the toilet facilities would be of more interest.

   *He ushers* PHILIP *and* VICKI *away from* MRS CLACKETT
   *towards the mezzanine bathroom.*

FLAVIA. Mrs Clackett, who are these people?

MRS CLACKETT. Oh, we get them all the time, love.
   They're just Arab sheets.

ROGER. I'm sorry about this.

   *He opens the door to the mezzanine bathroom.*

   But in here . . .

FLAVIA. *Arab* sheets?

   *Exit* FLAVIA *into the bedroom.*
   *Enter the* BURGLAR *from the mezzanine bathroom.*

ROGER. In here we have . . .

BURGLAR. Ballcocks, governor. Your ballcocks have gone.

ROGER. Oh, we have him.

   *Enter* FLAVIA *from the bedroom.*

FLAVIA. They're *Irish* sheets! Irish linen sheets off my own
   bed!

MRS CLACKETT. Oh, the thieving devils!

ROGER. In the *study*, however . . .

MRS CLACKETT. You give me that sheet, you devil!

*She seizes the nearest sheet, and it comes away in her hand to reveal* VICKI.

Oh, and there she stands in her smalls, for all the world to see!

ROGER. It's you!

FLAVIA. It's her!

FLAVIA *comes downstairs menacingly.*
*Exit* PHILIP *discreetly into the study.*

BURGLAR. It's my little girl!

VICKI. Dad!

FLAVIA *stops.*
*Enter* PHILIP *from the study in amazement. (He is now played by a double.)*

BURGLAR  Our little Vicki, that ran away from home, I thought I'd never see again!

MRS CLACKETT. Well, would you believe it?

VICKI (*to* BURGLAR): What are you doing here like this?

BURGLAR. What are *you* doing here like *that*?

VICKI. Me? I'm taking our files on tax evasion to Inland Revenue in Basingstoke.

PHILIP *collapses behind the sofa, clutching at his heart, unnoticed by the others.*

FLAVIA (*threateningly*): So where's my other sheet?

*Enter through the front door the most sought-after of all properties on the market today — a* SHEIKH.
*He is wearing Arab robes, and bears a strong resemblance to* PHILIP, *since he is played by the same actor.*

SHEIKH. Ah! A house of heavenly peace! I rent it!

OMNES. You!

FLAVIA. Is it?

FREDERICK. Lloyd, sorry, but I've still got my trousers round my ankles. It's just frightfully difficult doing a quick-change without a dresser.

LLOYD. Get Tim to help you. Tim! Where's Tim? Come on, Tim! Tim!

TIM, *wearing the sheet as* PHILIP's *double, gets to his feet and gazes blearily at* LLOYD.

TIM. Sorry?

LLOYD. Oh, yes. You're acting.

TIM. I must have dropped off down there.

LLOYD. Never mind, Tim.

TIM. Do something?

LLOYD. No, let it pass. We'll just struggle through on our own. Tim has a sleep behind the sofa, while all the rest of us run round with our trousers round our ankles. OK, Freddie? From your entrance, *with* trousers round ankles. 'So where's my other sheet.'

FREDERICK *hesitates.*

Some other problem, Freddie?

FREDERICK. Well, since we're stopped anyway.

LLOYD. Why did I ask?

FREDERICK. I mean, you know how stupid I am about plot.

LLOYD. I know, Freddie.

FREDERICK. May I ask another silly question?

LLOYD. All my studies in world drama lie at your disposal, Freddie.

FREDERICK. I still don't understand why the Sheikh just happens to be Philip's double.

GARRY. Because he comes in and we all think he's, you know, and we all, I mean, that's the joke.

FREDERICK. I see that.

BELINDA. My sweet, the rest of the plot depends on it!

FREDERICK. I see that. But it *is* rather a coincidence, isn't it?

LLOYD. It *is* rather a coincidence, Freddie, yes. Until you reflect that there was an earlier draft of the play, now unfortunately lost to us. And in this the author makes it clear that Philip's father as a young man had travelled extensively in the Middle East.

FREDERICK. I see . . . I *see*!

LLOYD. You see?

FREDERICK. That's very interesting.

LLOYD. I thought you'd like that.

FREDERICK. But will the audience get it?

LLOYD. You must tell them, Freddie. Looks. Gestures. That's what acting's all about. OK?

FREDERICK. Yes. Thank you, Lloyd. Thank you.

LLOYD. Right, can we just finish the act? From your entrance, Freddie.

*Exit* PHILIP *through the front door.*

God, I'm being so clever out here! What's going to be left of this show when I've gone back to London and you're up there on your own? 'So where's my other sheet?'

FLAVIA (*threateningly*): So where's my other sheet?

*Enter the* SHEIKH *through the front door.*

SHEIKH. Ah! A house of heavenly peace! I rent it!

OMNES. You!

FLAVIA. Is it?

SHEIKH (*with dignity*): Is me? Certainly is me! Who else?

*They all fall upon him.*

ROGER. You walk in asking to view a house like this, when you're nothing but a trouserless tramp! (*He pulls up the* SHEIKH's *robes.*)

SHEIKH. What?

MRS CLACKETT. You take all the clean sheets! (*Tries to pull the robes off him.*)

SHEIKH. What? What?

VICKI. You snatch my nightdress! (*Tries to pull his burnous off him.*)

FLAVIA. You toss me aside like a broken china doll! (*She hits him.*)

SHEIKH. What? What? What?

BURGLAR. And what you're up to with my little girl down there in Basingstoke I won't ask. But I'll tell you one thing, Vicki.

*Pause.*

LLOYD. Brooke!

BROOKE. Sorry . . .

LLOYD. Your line. Come on, love, we're two lines away from the end of the act.

BROOKE. I don't understand.

LLOYD. Give her the line!

BELINDA (*to* BROOKE): 'What's that, Dad?'

BROOKE. Yes, but I don't understand.

DOTTY. It's 'What's that, Dad?'

SELSDON. Yes, I say to you, 'I'll tell you one thing, Vicki,' and you say to me, 'What's that, Dad?'

BROOKE. I don't understand why the Sheikh looks like Philip.

*Silence. Everyone waits for the storm.*

LLOYD. Poppy! Bring the book!

*Enter* POPPY *from the wings, with the book.*

Is that the line, Poppy? 'I don't understand why the Sheikh looks like Philip?' Can we consult the author's text, and make absolutely sure?

POPPY. Well, I think it's . . .

LLOYD (*comes up on stage*): 'What's that, Dad?' Right. That's the line, Brooke, love. We all know you've worked in very classy places up in London where they let you make the play up as you go along, but we don't want that kind of thing here, love, not when the author has provided us with such a considered and polished line of his own, not at one o'clock in the morning, not two lines away from the end of Act One, not when we're just about to get a tea-break before we all drop dead of exhaustion. We merely want to hear the line. 'What's that, Dad?' That's all. Nothing else. I'm not being unreasonable, am I?

BROOKE *abruptly turns, runs upstairs, and exits into the mezzanine bathroom.*

Exit? Does it say 'exit'?

*The sound of* BROOKE *weeping, off, and running downstairs.*

Oh God, now she's going to wash her lenses away.

*Exit* LLOYD *through the front door.*

FREDERICK (*chastened*): Oh dear.

SELSDON (*likewise*): A little heavy with the sauce, I thought.

GARRY. I thought it was going to be Poppy when he finally, you know.

DOTTY. It's usually Poppy. Isn't it, love?

POPPY *smiles wryly.*

FREDERICK. I suppose that was all my fault.

GARRY. But why pick on, you know?

DOTTY. Yes, why Brooke?

BELINDA. I thought it was quite sweet, actually.

GARRY. Sweet?

BELINDA. A little lovers' tiff, really.

DOTTY. What, you mean, Lloyd and Brooke . . .?

BELINDA. Didn't you know?

SELSDON. Brooke and Lloyd?

BELINDA. Where do you think they've been all weekend?

FREDERICK. Good God. You mean, that's why he didn't realise they'd put the set up wrong on Sunday . . .?

BELINDA. Sh! Here they come!

*Enter* LLOYD *with his arm round* BROOKE.

LLOYD. OK. All forgotten. I was irresistible.

POPPY. I think I'm going to be sick.

*Exit* POPPY *into the wings.*

LLOYD. What?

DOTTY. Oh, no!

LLOYD. Oh, God!

*Exit* LLOYD *after* POPPY.

GARRY. You mean . . .?

SELSDON. Her, too?

FREDERICK. Oh, dear.

BELINDA. Well, that's something I *didn't* know.

BROOKE. I think I'm going to faint.

DOTTY. Yes, sit down, love!

BELINDA. Head between your knees, my precious.

*They sit* BROOKE *down with her head between her knees.*

SELSDON. Well, that's something *she* didn't know!

BELINDA. Hush, love.

DOTTY. Two weeks' rehearsal, that's all we've had.

FREDERICK. Whatever next?

SELSDON. *Most* exciting!

BELINDA. Sh! (*Indicates* BROOKE.)

SELSDON. Oh, yes. Sh!

DOTTY. Here he comes.

*Enter* LLOYD *from the wings, subdued.*

Is she all right, love?

LLOYD. She'll be all right in a minute. Something she ate, probably.

GARRY (*indicates* BROOKE): Yes, this one's feeling a bit, you know.

LLOYD. I'm feeling a bit, you know, myself. I think I'm going to . . .

BELINDA. Which?

GARRY (*offers chair*): Faint?

BELINDA (*offers vase*): Or be sick?

LLOYD. . . . Need that tea-break.

DOTTY. You're certainly overdoing it at the moment, love.

LLOYD. So could we just have the last line of the act?

SELSDON. Me? Last line? Right. 'But I'll tell you one thing, Vicki.'

> VICKI. What's that, Dad?
>
> BURGLAR. When all around is strife and uncertainty, there's nothing like . . .
>
> *He takes* MRS CLACKETT's *plate.*
>
> . . . a good old-fashioned plate of sardines!

LLOYD. And *curtain!*

*Pause. Then TIM realises, and hobbles hurriedly into the wings.*

**Curtain.**

**ACT ONE**

> *The living-room of the Brents' country home. Wednesday*
> *afternoon. (Theatre Royal, Goole. Wednesday matinee,*
> *February 13.)*

*But this time we are watching the act from behind; the whole set*
*has been turned through 180 degrees. All the doors can be seen —*
*there is no masking behind them. Two stairways lead up to the*
*platform which gives access to the doors on the upper levels.*
*Some of the scene inside the living-room is visible through the*
*full-length window. There are also two doors in the backstage*
*fabric of the theatre: one giving access to the dressing-rooms, and*
*the pass door into the auditorium. TIM is walking up and down*
*anxiously in his dinner jacket. POPPY is speaking into the*
*microphone in the prompt corner.*

POPPY (*over the Tannoy*): Act One beginners, please. Your calls,
Miss Otley, Miss Ashton, Mr Lejeune, Mr Fellowes, Miss Blair.
Act One beginners, please.

TIM. And maybe Act One beginners is what we'll get. What do
you think?

POPPY (*to* TIM): Oh, she'll pull herself together now we've
called Beginners. Now she knows she's got to be on stage in
five minutes. Won't she?

TIM. Will she?

POPPY. You know what Dotty's like.

TIM. We've only been on the road for a month! We've only got
to Goole! What's it going to be like by the time we've got to
Stockton-on-Tees?

POPPY. If only she'd speak!

TIM. If only she'd unlock the door! Look, if Dotty *won't* go on . . .

POPPY. Won't go on?

TIM. *If* she won't.

POPPY. She will.

TIM. Of course she will.

POPPY. Won't she?

TIM. I'm sure she will. But if she *doesn't* . . .

POPPY. She must!

TIM. She will, she will. But if she *didn't* . . .

POPPY. I'd have five minutes to change. Four minutes.

TIM. If only she'd say something.

*The pass door opens cautiously, and* LLOYD *puts his head round. He closes it again at the sight of* POPPY.

POPPY. I'll have another go. Takes your mind off your own problems, anyway.

*Exit* POPPY *in the direction of the dressing-rooms.*
LLOYD *puts his head back round the door.*

LLOYD. Has she gone?

TIM. Lloyd! I didn't know you were coming down today!

LLOYD *comes in. He is carrying a bottle of whisky.*

LLOYD. I wasn't. I haven't.

TIM. Anyway, thank God you're here!

LLOYD. I'm not.

TIM. Dotty and Garry . . .

LLOYD. I don't want anyone to know I'm in.

TIM. No, but Dotty and Garry . . .

LLOYD (*gives him the bottle*): Hide this somewhere.

TIM. Right. They've had some kind of row . . .

LLOYD (*takes money out of his wallet and gives it to* TIM). There's

a flower-shop just across the road at the back. I want you to
buy me some very large and expensive-looking flowers.

TIM. Right. Now Dotty's locked herself up in her dressing-room . . .

LLOYD. Don't let Poppy see them.

TIM. No. And she won't speak to anyone . . .

LLOYD. First house finishes just after five, yes? Second house
starts at seven-thirty? I want two hours alone and undisturbed
with Brooke in her dressing-room between the shows, then
I'm on the 7.25 back to London.

TIM. Lloyd, that's what I'm trying to tell you — there may not
*be* a show!

LLOYD. She hasn't walked out already?

TIM. No one knows what she's doing! She's locked in her
dressing-room! She won't speak to anyone!

LLOYD. You've called Beginners?

TIM. Yes!

LLOYD. I can't do it in five minutes. It's not physiologically possible.

TIM. She's had bust-ups with Garry before, of course.

LLOYD. Brooke's had a bust-up with *Garry*?

TIM. Brooke? Not Brooke — Dotty!

LLOYD. Oh, Dotty.

TIM. I mean, they had the famous bust-up the week before last,
when we were playing Worksop.

LLOYD. Right, right, you told me on the phone.

TIM. She went out with this journalist bloke . . .

LLOYD. Journalist — yes, yes . . .

TIM. But you know Garry threatened to kill him?

LLOYD. Killed him, yes, I know. Listen, don't worry about
Dotty — she's got money in the show.

TIM. Yes, but now it's happened again! Two o'clock this
morning I'm woken up by this great banging on my door.

It's Garry. Do I know where Dotty is? — She hasn't come home.

LLOYD. Tim, let me tell you something about *my* life. I have the Duke of Buckingham on the phone to me for an hour after rehearsal every evening complaining that the Duke of Gloucester is sucking boiled sweets through his speeches. Catesby is off every afternoon doing a telly, and the Duke of Clarence is off for the entire week doing a commercial for Madeira. Richard himself — would you believe? — Richard III has now gone down with a back problem. Then last night Brooke rings me to say she's very unhappy here, and she's got herself a doctor's certificate for nervous exhaustion. I have no time to find or rehearse another Vicki. I have just one afternoon, while Richard is fitted for a surgical corset and Lady Anne starts divorce proceedings, to cure Brooke of nervous exhaustion, with no medical aids except a little whisky — you've got the whisky? — a few flowers — you've got the money for the flowers? — and a certain fading bedside manner. So I haven't come to the theatre to hear about other people's problems. I've come to be taken out of myself, and preferably not put back again.

TIM. Yes, but Lloyd . . .

LLOYD. Have you done the front of house calls?

TIM. Oh, the front of house calls!

*TIM hurries to the microphone in the prompt corner, still holding the money and whisky. He puts the whisky down to switch on the microphone.*

LLOYD. And don't let Poppy see those flowers!

*Exit LLOYD through the pass door.*

TIM (*into microphone*): Ladies and gentlemen, will you please take your seats. The curtain will rise in three minutes.

*Enter POPPY from the dressing-rooms.*

POPPY. We're going to be so late up!

TIM. No luck?

POPPY. Belinda's having a go. I haven't even started the front of house calls yet . . . Money? Is this for me?

TIM. No, no! (*He puts the money behind his back and automatically produces the whisky with his other hand.*)

POPPY. Whisky!

TIM. Oh . . . Is it?

POPPY. Where did you find that?

TIM. Well . . .

POPPY. Not up here? Oh, my God, he's hiding them up here now! (*She takes the whisky.*) I'll put it downstairs where he won't find it.

*Enter* BELINDA *from the dressing-rooms.*

No?

BELINDA. You know what Dotty's like when she's like this. Freddie's trying now . . . (*She sees the whisky.*) Oh, my God.

POPPY. He's hiding them up here now.

*Enter* FREDERICK *from the dressing-rooms.*

No?

FREDERICK. No.

BELINDA. You didn't try for very long, my precious!

FREDERICK. No, well . . . (*He sees the whisky.*) Oh dear.

BELINDA. He's hiding them up here now.

*Exit* POPPY *to the dressing-rooms, holding the whisky.*

FREDERICK. No, Garry came rushing out of his dressing-room in a great state. I couldn't quite understand what he was saying. I often feel with Garry that I must have missed something somewhere. You know how stupid I am about that kind of thing. But I think he was saying he wanted to kill me.

BELINDA. Oh, my poor sweet!

FREDERICK. I thought I'd better leave him to it. I don't want to make things worse. He's all right, is he?

BELINDA. Who, Garry? Anything but, by the sound of it!

FREDERICK. I mean, he's going on?

TIM. Garry? *Garry's* going on. Of course he's going on. What's all this about Garry not going on?

BELINDA. Yes, because if you have to go on for Garry, Poppy can't go on for Dotty, because if Poppy goes on for Dotty, you'll have to be on the corner!

TIM. Oh my God.

*He taps his left hand anxiously with the money in his right.*

BELINDA. Money.

TIM. Money?

BELINDA. Is that for us?

TIM. No, that's for . . . Oh, my God!

*Exit* TIM *to the dressing-rooms.*

FREDERICK. She's a funny woman, you know — Dotty. So up and down. She was perfectly all right last night.

BELINDA. Last night?

FREDERICK. Yes, she took me for a drink after the show in some club she knows about.

BELINDA. She was with *you*? *You* were with *her*?

FREDERICK. She was being very sympathetic about all my troubles.

BELINDA. She's not going to sink her teeth into you! I won't let her!

FREDERICK. No, no, she couldn't have been nicer. In fact she came back to my digs afterwards for a cup of tea, and she told me all *her* troubles. Sat there until three o'clock this morning — I don't know what the landlady thought!

*Enter* POPPY.

POPPY. And another thing.

BELINDA. Nothing else, my sweet!

POPPY. Where's Selsdon?

BELINDA. It turns out that it's Freddie here who's the cause of all the . . . Selsdon?

POPPY. He's not in his dressing-room.

BELINDA. Oh my God!

POPPY. Oh my God, the front of house calls!

BELINDA. You do the calls. I'll look for Selsdon.

FREDERICK. What shall *I* do?

BELINDA (*firmly*): Absolutely nothing at all.

FREDERICK. Right.

BELINDA. You've done quite enough already, my pet.

*Exit* BELINDA *to the dressing-rooms.*

POPPY (*into the microphone*): Ladies and gentlemen, will you please take your seats. The curtain will rise in three minutes.

*Enter* TIM *from the dressing-rooms, carrying a large bunch of flowers.*

TIM. He wants to kill someone.

POPPY. *Selsdon* wants to kill someone?

TIM. Garry, Garry . . . Selsdon?

POPPY. We've lost him.

TIM. Oh my God.

POPPY. Flowers!

TIM (*embarrassed*). Oh . . . Well . . . They're just . . . You know . . .

POPPY (*takes them*). Oh, Tim, that's really sweet of you!

TIM. Oh . . . Well . . .

POPPY (*to* FREDERICK). Isn't that sweet of him?

FREDERICK. Very charming.

*She kisses* TIM.

POPPY. I'll just look in the pub. (*She gives the flowers to* FREDERICK.) Hold these.

*Exit* POPPY *to the dressing-rooms.*

TIM. I'll take those. (*Takes the flowers.*) Oh, the front of house calls! Hold these. (*Gives the flowers back to* FREDERICK.)

FREDERICK. Oh, I think Poppy's done them.

TIM. She gave them two minutes, did she? I'll give them one minute. (*Into the microphone.*) Ladies and gentlemen, will you please take your seats. The curtain will rise in one minute.

*Takes the flowers from* FREDERICK.

FREDERICK. Oh dear, I think she said three minutes.

TIM. *Three* minutes? *I* said three minutes! *She* said three minutes?

FREDERICK. I think so.

TIM. Hold these. (*Gives* FREDERICK *the flowers. Into microphone.*) Ladies and gentlemen, will you please take your seats. The curtain will rise in two minutes.

*Enter* BELINDA *from the dressing-rooms, holding the bottle of whisky.*

FREDERICK. Any luck?

BELINDA. No, but I found this.

FREDERICK. Oh dear.

TIM. Oh . . .

BELINDA. It was quite cunningly hidden behind the fire-extinguishers.

FREDERICK. *Not* a good sign.

TIM. I'll take it.

BELINDA. Yes, and put it somewhere out of sight, my sweet!

*Enter* POPPY *from the dressing-rooms.* TIM *conceals the whisky from her.*

POPPY. He's not in the pub.

TIM. You've checked the green room?

BELINDA. Yes.

TIM. I'll check it again.

*Exit* TIM *to the dressing-rooms, with the whisky.*

BELINDA. Now what?

POPPY (*into the microphone*): Ladies and gentlemen, will you please take your seats. The curtain will rise in two minutes.

FREDERICK. Oh dear. Tim's already told them two minutes.

POPPY. He's done two minutes? (*Into the microphone.*) Ladies and gentlemen, will you please take your seats. The curtain will rise in one minute.

*Enter* LLOYD *through the pass door.*

LLOYD. What the fuck is going on?

BELINDA. Lloyd!

FREDERICK. Great Scott!

POPPY. I didn't know you were here!

LLOYD. I'm *not* here! I'm in London! But I can't sit out there and listen to 'two minutes' — 'three minutes' — 'one minute' — 'two minutes'!

BELINDA. My sweet, we're having great dramas downstairs!

LLOYD. We're having great dramas out there! (*To* POPPY:) This is the matinee, honey! There's old-age pensioners out there! 'The curtain will rise in three minutes' — we all start for the Gents. 'The curtain will rise in one minute' — we all come running out again. We don't know *which* way we're going!

POPPY. Lloyd, I've got to have a talk to you.

LLOYD (*kisses her mechanically*): Just tell me one thing, honey.

POPPY. I tried phoning you.

LLOYD. Is Brooke going on?

BELINDA. Is *Brooke* going on?

*Enter* BROOKE *from the dressing-rooms, with the whisky.*

Brooke! You're going on, aren't you?

BROOKE. Sorry?

FREDERICK. Are you all right, Brooke?

BROOKE. Am I all right?

LLOYD. Fine. OK. She sounds like her usual self to me.

BROOKE. Lloyd?

LLOYD (*kisses her, and sees the whisky*): What's this?

BELINDA. Another one?

BROOKE. I was lying on the floor of the green room . . .

LLOYD. You were lying on the floor of the green room?

BELINDA. For her relaxation.

LLOYD. Oh yes.

BROOKE. And I saw it hidden behind the radiator.

BELINDA. Oh my God, he's hiding them everywhere!

FREDERICK (*takes the whisky*): I'll put it where he won't find it.

LLOYD. Put it in Brooke's dressing-room. He won't think of looking in . . . (*Sees the flowers that* FREDERICK *is holding.*) What's *this*?

FREDERICK. Oh, yes, sorry. (*He gives the flowers to* POPPY.)

POPPY. Tim bought them for me. (*She puts them on her desk in the prompt corner.*)

LLOYD. *Tim*? Bought them for *you*?

POPPY. Lloyd, there's something I've got to tell you.

LLOYD. I've heard everything I want to hear for today. (*Goes towards the pass door.*)

BELINDA. But what about Dotty?

LLOYD. No.

FREDERICK. And Garry?

LLOYD. No.

BELINDA. What about Selsdon?

LLOYD. Listen, I think this show is beyond the help of a director. You just do it. I'll sit out there in the dark with a bag of toffees and enjoy it. OK? 'One minute' was the last call, if your memory goes back that far.

*Exit* LLOYD *through the pass door.*
BROOKE *lies down on the floor.*

FREDERICK. *Is* she all right?

BELINDA. It's her relaxation, my precious. (*To* BROOKE:) You *are* all right, aren't you, my love?

BROOKE. Yes. I couldn't concentrate downstairs. Everyone seemed to be shouting and running around somehow.

BELINDA (*to* FREDERICK): It's her breathing, you see.

FREDERICK. Oh dear. (*To* BROOKE:) You don't have to go on, you know, if you're not feeling up to it. It's only the matinee. I'm sure Poppy would always be delighted to have a bash on your behalf. Wouldn't you, Poppy?

POPPY. I'll see what's happening downstairs.

*Exit* POPPY *to the dressing-rooms.*

BELINDA. Freddie, my sweet precious . . .

FREDERICK. What? Did I say something wrong?

*Enter* SELSDON *hurriedly through the pass door.*

SELSDON. Where's Tim?

BELINDA. Selsdon! My sweet! Where have you been?

FREDERICK. Are you all right? (*Puts out a sympathetic hand, then realises that it contains the whisky bottle.*) Oh dear. (*Hurriedly puts it out of sight behind his back.*)

BELINDA. We've been looking for you everywhere!

SELSDON. Oh, yes, everywhere. In front — manager's office — bar — not a sign of him.

BELINDA. He's looking for you, downstairs.

SELSDON. That's right! Great shindig been going on down there. I thought Tim ought to know about it.

BELINDA. My love, I think he's heard.

SELSDON. Oh, everything! Oh, he really went for her! 'I know when you've got your eye on someone!' he says. 'I've seen the way you've been looking at Teddy.'

BELINDA. Oh my God.

FREDERICK. Teddy? Who's Teddy?

BELINDA. Oh, Freddie, can't you guess?

FREDERICK. Teddy?

SELSDON. Or it may have been Neddy.

BELINDA. Oh, poor Neddy!

SELSDON. Yes, Teddy or Neddy. One of the two. Anyway . . .

*Enter* POPPY *from the dressing-rooms.*

POPPY. I think they're coming.

BELINDA. They're coming!

FREDERICK. They're coming!

SELSDON. I knew they wouldn't.

POPPY. And you're *here*!

SELSDON. Oh, yes, every word!

POPPY. Right. (*Into the microphone.*) Ladies and gentlemen, will you please take your seats. The performance is about to begin.

*Enter* TIM *from the dressing-rooms.*

TIM. They're coming.

BELINDA. And we've found Selsdon.

TIM (*to* SELSDON): How did you get here?

SELSDON. How?

TIM (*into microphone*): Ladies and gentlemen, will you please take your seats.

POPPY. I've done it, I've done it!

TIM (*into microphone*): The performance is . . . oh.

BELINDA. Poor Lloyd! He'll choke on his toffees.

SELSDON. You want to know how? Amiss, that's how!

TIM. What?

SELSDON. How did she take it? In one word? Amiss! 'It's always the same thing,' she cries.

*Enter* GARRY *from the dressing-rooms.*

BELINDA. Garry, my sweet!

SELSDON. 'You try to give some poor devil a leg up.' Or she may have said, 'a leg over . . .' Oh, and here he is.

FREDERICK (*to* GARRY): Are you all right?

FREDERICK *collects the box and flight bag from the props table, and offers them to* GARRY, *who snatches them angrily.*

SELSDON. What does he say?

BELINDA. He's not saying anything, Selsdon, my sweet.

SELSDON. Very sensible. Only stir it up again. 'I've seen you at it!' — that's what he kept saying downstairs.

*Enter* DOTTY *from the dressing-rooms.*

'I know when you've got your claws into someone,' he says, 'and you've got them into poor old Neddy!'

BELINDA. Dotty, my love!

SELSDON. Oh, she's emerged, has she? Come on, old girl! You're on!

FREDERICK. Are you all right?

SELSDON. Is she all right?

DOTTY *merely sighs, and smiles, and gives a little squeeze of the arm to* BELINDA. *She takes up her place by the service quarters entrance, a tragically misunderstood woman.* GARRY *moves pointedly away.*

BELINDA (*to* SELSDON): She's fine.

TIM. All right, everyone?

SELSDON. Or maybe it was Eddy. Neddy or Eddy — one of the two.

BELINDA. Hush, love.

POPPY. Curtain up?

*Everyone looks anxiously from* DOTTY *to* GARRY *and back again.* DOTTY *and* GARRY *both ignore the looks. They stand aloof, then both, at the same moment, turn to check their appearance in the little mirrors fixed to the back of the set.*

FREDERICK. Look, Dotty — look, Garry — I'm not going to make a great speech, but we *have* all got to go out there and put on a performance, and, well . . .

BELINDA. We can't do it in silence, my loves! We're going to have to speak to each other!

*Pause. Neither* GARRY *nor* DOTTY *has apparently heard.*

DOTTY (*suddenly, to* TIM): What's the house like?

BELINDA. That's the spirit!

FREDERICK. Well done, Dotty!

TIM. It's quite good. Well, for a matinee.

POPPY. There's quite a crowd at the front of the back stalls.

SELSDON (*to* POPPY): Come on, girl, get the tabs up! Some of those OAPs out there haven't got long to go.

POPPY. Right. Quiet, then, please . . .

FREDERICK. Let me just say one word . . . Hold it a moment, Poppy . . .

SELSDON. Let *me* just say one word. Sardines!

BELINDA. Sardines!

FREDERICK. Sardines!

BELINDA *rushes to the prop table to fetch* DOTTY *the plate of sardines that she takes on for her first entrance.*

POPPY (*over Tannoy*): Quiet on stage. House lights going down. Act One . . .

*Enter* LLOYD *through the pass door.*

LLOYD. *Now* what?

TIM. We're just going up.

LLOYD. We've been sitting there for an hour! They've gone quiet! They think someone's died!

FREDERICK. I'm sorry, Lloyd. It's my fault. I was just saying a few words to everyone.

LLOYD. Freddie, have you ever thought of having a brain transplant?

FREDERICK. Sorry, sorry. Wrong moment. I see that.

LLOYD. Anybody else have thoughts they feel they must communicate?

POPPY. Well, not now, of course, but . . .

LLOYD. *What?*

POPPY. I mean, you know, later . . .

LLOYD (*to* TIM). And you bought those flowers for Poppy?

TIM. No . . . well . . . yes . . .

LLOYD. And you didn't buy any flowers for me?

TIM. No . . . well . . . no . . .

LLOYD. Tim, have you ever heard of such a thing as jealous rage?

TIM. Yes . . . well . . . yes . . .

LLOYD. Then take five pounds of your own money, Tim, and go out to the florists and buy some flowers for *me*! Gave Poppy the flowers! You two could have Freddie's old brain — you could have half each.

*Exit* LLOYD *through the pass door.*

FREDERICK. Oh dear.

BELINDA. Don't cry, Poppy, love.

SELSDON. Just get the old bus on the road.

POPPY (*over Tannoy*): Act One. Curtain up.

*She presses a buzzer, and the act begins. (Note: the act that follows is a somewhat condensed version of the one we saw rehearsed.)*

> *As the curtain rises, the award-winning modern telephone is ringing.*

DOTTY *makes her entrance.*
*There is a sound of*
*scattered applause.*

SELSDON, BELINDA *and*
FREDERICK *express silent*
*relief that the show has at*
*last started. They subside*
*on to the chairs.*

TIM *takes his wallet and*
*checks his money.*
*He goes to exit, but*
*stops and turns when*
BELINDA *points out to the*
*others* GARRY *sighing*
*heavily as he waits for his*
*entrance.* FREDERICK
*puts the whisky down on*
*his chair and goes across to*
GARRY. BELINDA *and*
TIM *watch apprehensively*
*as* FREDERICK *gives*
GARRY'*s arm a silently*
*sympathetic squeeze.*

GARRY *shakes him off*
*indignantly.*

*Enter from the service*
*quarters* MRS CLACKETT,
*a housekeeper of character.*
*She is carrying an imposing*
*plate of sardines.*

MRS CLACKETT. It's no
good you going on. I can't
open sardines *and* answer
the phone. I've only got
one pair of hands. (*She puts*
*the sardines on the tele-*
*phone table by the sofa,*
*and picks up the phone.*)
Hello . . . Yes, but there's
no one here, love . . . No,
Mr Brent's not here . . . He
lives here, yes, but he don't
live here now because he
lives in Spain . . . Mr Philip
Brent, that's right . . . The
one that writes the plays,
that's him, only now he
writes them in Spain . . .
No, she's in Spain, too,
they're all in Spain, there's
no one here . . . Am I in
Spain? No, I'm not in Spain,
dear. I look after the house
for them, only I go home
at one o'clock on
Wednesday, so that's where
*I* am . . . No, because I've
got a nice plate of sardines
to put my feet up with, and
they've got colour here, and
it's the royal what's it called
— the royal you know —
where's the paper, then . . .?

BELINDA *hurries across to draw* FREDERICK *off.*

FREDERICK *cannot understand what he has done to cause offence. He demonstrates what he did by giving* GARRY's *arm another squeeze.*

GARRY *drops his props and threatens to hit* FREDERICK.

FREDERICK *covers his nose.* BELINDA *and* TIM *separate them, and urge* GARRY *back to the front door.* TIM *goes off towards the dressing-rooms.*

*She searches in the newspaper.*

. . . And if it's to do with letting the house then you'll have to ring the house-agents, because they're the agents for the house . . . Squire, Squire, Hackham and who's the other one . . .? No, they're not in Spain, they're next to the phone in the study. Squire, Squire, Hackham, and hold on, I'll go and look.

*She replaces the receiver.*

Always the same, isn't it. Soon as you take the weight off your feet, down it all comes on your head.

*Exit* MRS CLACKETT *into the study, still holding the newspaper.*
*The sound of a key in the lock. The front door opens. On the doorstep stands* ROGER, *holding a card-board box. He is about thirty, and has the well-appointed air of a man who handles high-class real estate.*

ROGER. . . . my housekeeper, yes, but this is her afternoon off.

BROOKE *makes her entrance.*

*Enter* VICKI *through the front door. She is a*

*desirable property in her
early twenties, well-built
and beautifully maintained
throughout.*

FREDERICK *gives* DOTTY
*a sympathetic squeeze of
the arm in her turn.*

ROGER. So we've got the
place entirely to ourselves.

*As* GARRY *turns back to
collect the flight bag he
gets a fleeting glimpse
of this.*

ROGER *goes back and
brings in a flight bag, and
closes the front door.*

I'll just check.

*As* GARRY *comes through
the service quarters door he
sees* BELINDA *glancing at
him and hurriedly discon-
necting* FREDERICK
*from* DOTTY. *He stamps
on* FREDERICK's *foot.*

*He opens the door to the
service quarters.* VICKI
*gazes round.*

Hello? Anyone at home?

FREDERICK *turns to*
BELINDA *and asks her
what's wrong. She finds it
difficult to explain with*
DOTTY *there.*

*Closes the door.*

No, there's no one here. So
what do you think?

VICKI. All these doors.

ROGER. Oh, only a handful,
really. Study. Kitchens, and
a self-contained service flat
for the housekeeper.

BELINDA *discovers that*
DOTTY *is now silently
pouring out her grievances
against* GARRY *to the
sympathetic* FREDERICK.

VICKI. Terrific. And which
one's the . . .?

ROGER. What?

VICKI. You know . . .

ROGER. Oh. Through here.

*Opens the downstairs
bathroom for her.*

BELINDA *only just manages to detach* DOTTY *and get her back on stage for her entrance.*

VICKI. Fantastic.

*Exit* VICKI *into the bathroom.*
*Enter* MRS CLACKETT *from the study, without the newspaper.*

MRS CLACKETT. Now I've lost the sardines . . .

*Mutual surprise.* ROGER *closes the door to the bathroom, and slips the champagne back into the bag.*

ROGER. I'm sorry. I thought there was no one here.

BELINDA *tries to explain to* FREDERICK *that* DOTTY *has taken a fancy to him.* FREDERICK *can't understand a word of it. She turns to* BROOKE *to ask her to explain to* FREDERICK *but she can't understand anything.*

MRS CLACKETT. I'm not here. I'm off, only it's the royal you know, where they wear those hats, and they're all covered in fruit.

ROGER. I'm from the agents. I just dropped in to . . . go into a few things. Well, to check some of the measurements. Do one or two odd jobs.

*The bathroom door opens.* ROGER *closes it.*

Oh, and a client. I'm showing a prospective tenant over the house.

BELINDA *suddenly points out that* SELSDON *has discovered the whisky*

VICKI (*off, opening the door*): What's wrong with this door?

ROGER. She's thinking of

*that* FREDERICK *left on the chair.* SELSDON *opens the bottle, smells it, closes it again, and then goes off to the dressing-rooms with it.*
FREDERICK *goes to run after* SELSDON. BELINDA *tells him to wait there — sit still — do absolutely nothing — while she runs after* SELSDON.
*Exit* BELINDA *in the direction of the dressing-rooms in pursuit of* SELSDON.

DOTTY *makes her exit, puts down the sardines, shaking her head with misery, and begins to weep.*

FREDERICK *is very agitated by this. He takes the sardines away from her, pats her on the shoulder, gives her a hand-kerchief, pushes the sardines back into her hand, and edges her towards*

renting it. Her interest is definitely aroused.

*Enter* VICKI *from bathroom.*

VICKI. That's not the bedroom.

ROGER. The bedroom? No, that's the downstairs bathroom and WC suite. And this is the housekeeper. Mrs Crockett.

MRS CLACKETT. Clackett, dear, Clackett. Only now I've lost the newspaper.

*Exit* MRS CLACKETT *into the study, carrying the sardines.*

ROGER. I'm sorry about this.

VICKI. That's all right. We don't want the television, do we?

ROGER. Only she's been in the family for generations.

VICKI. Great. Come on, then. (*Starts upstairs.*) I've got to be in Basingstoke by four.

ROGER. Perhaps we should just have a glass of champagne.

VICKI. We'll take it up with us.

ROGER. Yes, Well . . .

VICKI. And don't let my files

*the door. At the last
moment she realises she
hasn't got the newspaper.
FREDERICK runs and
fetches it from the props
table. Then she realises
that she has still got the
sardines.*

*He gets them off her just
in time for her to make
her entrance.*

*Enter BELINDA from the
dressing-rooms leading a
bewildered SELSDON, but
without the whisky.
FREDERICK tells her what
a terrible state DOTTY is
in.*

*They turn to watch her
anxiously as she makes*

out of sight.

ROGER. No. Only . . .

VICKI. What?

ROGER. Well . . .

VICKI. Her?

ROGER. She has been in the
family for generations.

*Enter MRS CLACKETT
from the study, with the
newspaper but without the
sardines.*

MRS CLACKETT. Sardines . . .
sardines . . . It's not for me
to say, of course, dear,
only I will just say this:
don't think twice about
it -- take the plunge. You'll
really enjoy it here.

VICKI. Oh. Great.

MRS CLACKETT (*to* ROGER):
Won't she, love?

ROGER. Yes. Well. Yes!

MRS CLACKETT (*to* VICKI):
And we'll enjoy having you
(*To* ROGER:) Won't we, love?

ROGER. Oh. Well.

VICKI. Terrific.

MRS CLACKETT. Sardines,
sardines. Can't put your
feet up on an empty
stomach, can you.

*her exit.*

SELSDON *seizes the opportunity to depart again to the dressing-rooms.*

BELINDA *runs after him.* FREDERICK *goes to accompany her, but turns anxiously back to reassure* DOTTY.

*But she is now smiling bravely, and telling him that she has pulled her-self together, thanks to him.* DOTTY *gives* FREDERICK *a kiss to express her gratitude.*

As GARRY *comes through door of mezzanine bath-room, he catches a fleeting glimpse of the kiss.*

FREDERICK *now realises that he has an entrance coming up with* BELINDA, *and no* BELINDA. *He urgently tries to persuade* DOTTY *to go off and find her.*

GARRY *appears in the linen cupboard doorway and takes a good look at the earnest colloquy between* FREDERICK

*Exit* MRS CLACKETT *to service quarters.*

VICKI. You see? She thinks it's great. She's even making us sardines!

ROGER. Well . . .

VICKI. I think she's terrific.

ROGER. Terrific.

VICKI. So which way?

ROGER (*picks up the bags*): All right. Before she comes back with the sardines.

VICKI. Up here?

ROGER. Yes, yes.

VICKI. In here?

ROGER. Yes, yes, yes.

*Exeunt* ROGER *and* VICKI *into mezzanine bathroom.*

VICKI. It's another bathroom.

*They reappear.*

ROGER. No, no, no.

VICKI . Always trying to get me into bathrooms.

ROGER. I mean in *here.*

*Nods at the next door — the first along the gallery.* VICKI *leads the way in.* ROGER *follows.*

VICKI. Oh, black sheets! (*Produces one.*)

ROGER. It's the airing

| | |
|---|---|
| *and* DOTTY. *He throws the sheet at them.* | cupboard. (*Throws the sheet back.*) This one, this one, this one. |

*He drops the bag and box, and struggles nervously to open the second door along the gallery, the bedroom.*

VICKI. Oh, you're in a real state!

ROGER. Come on, then.

VICKI. You can't even get the door open.

*Exeunt* ROGER *and* VICKI *into the bedroom.*

*The sound of a key in the lock, and the front door opens. On the doorstep stands* PHILIP, *carrying a cardboard box. He is in his forties, with a deep suntan, and writes attractive new plays with a charming period atmosphere.*

BELINDA *enters from the dressing-rooms, holding the bottle of whisky.*

PHILIP. . . . Yes, but this is Mrs Clackett's afternoon off.

*She gives the whisky to* DOTTY, *and just makes her entrance.*

*Enter* FLAVIA. *She is in her thirties, the perfect companion piece to the above.*

*Enter* SELSDON *from the dressing-rooms.*

We've got the place entirely to ourselves.

*He asks* DOTTY *for the whisky.*

PHILIP *brings in a flight bag and closes the door.*

*But she is distracted by GARRY, who tells her that he will no longer tolerate these furtive meetings with FREDERICK.*

SELSDON *tries urgently to get the whisky off them as they quarrel.*

GARRY *and* DOTTY *both turn on him in fury.*

GARRY *pleads with* DOTTY — *kneels — weeps — hangs on to her plate of sardines.*

DOTTY *breaks away from*

FLAVIA. Look at it!

PHILIP. Do you like it?

FLAVIA. I can't believe it!

PHILIP. The perfect place for an assignation.

FLAVIA. Home.

PHILIP. Home.

FLAVIA. Our little secret hideaway.

PHILIP. The last place on earth anyone will look for us.

FLAVIA. It's rather funny, creeping in like this. I wonder if Mrs Clackett's aired the beds.

PHILIP. Darling!

FLAVIA. Well, why not? No children. No friends dropping in. We're absolutely on our own.

PHILIP. True. (*Picks up the bag and box and ushers* FLAVIA *towards the stairs.*) There is something to be said for being a tax exile.

FLAVIA. Leave those!

*He drops the bag and box and kisses her. She flees upstairs, laughing, and he after her.*

PHILIP. Sh!

FLAVIA. What?

GARRY. SELSDON *points out that she is still holding the whisky.*
GARRY *takes it off her as she makes her entrance.*

PHILIP. Inland Revenue may hear us!

*They creep to the bedroom door.*

*Enter* MRS CLACKETT *from the service quarters carrying a fresh plate of sardines.*

SELSDON *tries to get the whisky off* GARRY, *but* GARRY *turns to ascend the platform for his entrance.*

MRS CLACKETT (*to herself*): What I did with that first lot of sardines I shall never know.

*She puts the sardines on the telephone table and sits on the sofa.*

*He looks round for some-thing to do with the whisky, and gives it to* BROOKE.

PHILIP *and* FLAVIA (*looking down from the gallery*): Mrs Clackett!

MRS CLACKETT *jumps up.*

BROOKE *peers at it, no idea what she's supposed to do with it.*

*She asks* SELSDON, *who wags a reproving finger at her for possessing such a dangerous substance, and takes it from her.*

MRS CLACKETT. Oh, you give me a turn! My heart jumped right out of my boots!

PHILIP. So did mine!

FLAVIA. We thought you'd gone!

MRS CLACKETT. I thought you was in Spain!

*Then he demonstrates to* BROOKE *pulling a chain, and points at himself.*

PHILIP. We are! We are!

FLAVIA. You haven't seen us!

BROOKE, *undressing for her next entrance, peers uncomprehendingly.*

PHILIP. We're not here!

MRS CLACKETT. You'll want your things, look.

*Exit* SELSDON *to the dressing-rooms with the whisky.*

(*Indicates the bag and box.*)

PHILIP. Oh. Yes. Thanks.

PHILIP *comes downstairs, and picks up the bag and box.*

MRS CLACKETT (*to FLAVIA*): Oh, and that bed hasn't been aired, love.

FLAVIA. I'll get a hot water bottle.

BELINDA *makes her exit.*

*Exit* FLAVIA *into the mezzanine bathroom.*

BROOKE *tells* BELINDA *that* SELSDON *is drinking.*

MRS CLACKETT. I've put all your letters in the study, dear.

PHILIP. Oh my God. Where are they?

MRS CLACKETT. I've put them all in the little pigeonhouse.

PHILIP. In the pigeonhouse?

MRS CLACKETT. In the little pigeonhouse in your desk, love.

GARRY, *still on the platform, tries to see what* DOTTY *and* FREDERICK *are doing, but is fetched back by* BROOKE *for his entrance.*

*Exeunt* MRS CLACKETT *and* PHILIP *into the study.* PHILIP *is still holding the bag and box.*

*Enter* ROGER *from the bedroom, still dressed, tying his tie.*

DOTTY *sees* GARRY *watching them, and explains to* FREDERICK *that* GARRY *now thinks*

ROGER. Yes, but I could hear voices!

*that* FREDERICK *is her
lover.
. . . By this time* BROOKE
*has to make her entrance.*

*Enter* VICKI *from the
bedroom in her underwear.*

VICKI. Voices? What sort of
voices?

ROGER. People's voices.

VICKI (*looks over the
bannisters*): Oh, look, she's
opened our sardines.

*She moves to go downstairs.*
ROGER *grabs her.*

ROGER. Come back!

VICKI. What?

ROGER. I'll fetch them! You
can't go downstairs like
that.

BELINDA *urgently passes
on the information about*
SELSDON's *drinking to*
DOTTY. *But by the time
she takes it in, it's time for
her entrance.*

VICKI. Why not?

ROGER. Mrs Crackett.

VICKI. Mrs Crackett?

ROGER. She's irreplaceable.

*Enter* MRS CLACKETT
*from the study. She is
carrying the first plate of
sardines.*

MRS CLACKETT (*to herself*):
Sardines here. Sardines
there. It's like a Sunday
school outing.

BROOKE *makes her exit.
and* BELINDA *runs up to
the platform to ask her
where* SELSDON *is.*

ROGER *pushes* VICKI
*through the first available
door, which happens to be
the linen cupboard.*

BROOKE *points in the direction of the dressing-rooms.*

*Enter* TIM *from the dressing-rooms with a second, smaller, bunch of flowers.*
*Exit* BELINDA *to the dressing-rooms in haste.*

TIM *asks* FREDERICK *where she is going.*

FREDERICK *demonstrates raising the elbow.*

*Enter* BELINDA *from the dressing-rooms.*
*She demonstrates that* SELSDON *has locked himself in somewhere.*

PHILIP *says his line.*

TIM *hands* BELINDA *the flowers, and dashes out to the dressing-rooms.*

Oh, you're still poking around, are you?

ROGER. Yes, still poking — well, still around.

MRS CLACKETT. In the airing cupboard, were you?

ROGER. No, no. (*The linen cupboard door begins to open. He slams it shut.*) Well, just checking the sheets and pillow-cases. Going through the inventory

*He starts downstairs.*

ROGER. Mrs Blackett . . .

MRS CLACKETT. Clackett, dear, Clackett.

*She puts down the sardines beside the other sardines.*

ROGER. Mrs Clackett. Is there anyone else in the house, Mrs Clackett?

MRS CLACKETT. I haven't seen no one, dear.

ROGER. I thought I heard voices.

MRS CLACKETT. Voices? There's no voices here, love.

ROGER. I must have imagined it.

PHILIP (*off*): Oh my God!

ROGER, *with his back to her, picks up both plates of sardines.*

*She gives the flowers to FREDERICK and fetches the fireman's axe from the fire point.*

*She is going to rush off to the dressing-rooms with it when POPPY reminds her that she has an entrance coming up. BELINDA runs up on to the platform, finds she is still holding the axe, and gives it to BROOKE.*

*But before she can explain what to do with it, BELINDA has to make her entrance.*

GARRY *advances threateningly upon* FREDERICK *and gazes suspiciously at the flowers he is holding.* FREDERICK *has to hand* GARRY *the flowers in order to make his entrance.*

BROOKE *comes down from the platform and asks* GARRY *what she is supposed to do with the axe.* GARRY *takes it thoughtfully, and puts the flowers into her hands. He looks at the axe, then whirls it up over his head to wait for* FREDERICK's *exit.*

ROGER. I beg your pardon?

MRS CLACKETT (*mimics* PHILIP): Oh my God!

ROGER. Why, what is it?

MRS CLACKETT. Oh my God, the study door's open.

*She crosses and closes it.* ROGER *looks out of the window.*

ROGER. There's another car outside! That's not Mr Hackham's, is it? Or Mr Dudleys?

*Exit* ROGER *through the front door, holding both plates of sardines.*

*Enter* FLAVIA *from the mezzanine bathroom, carrying a hot water bottle. She sees the linen cupboard door open as she passes, pushes it shut, and turns the key.*

FLAVIA. Nothing but flapping doors in this house.

*Exit* FLAVIA *into the bedroom.*
*Enter from the study* PHILIP, *holding a tax demand and its envelope.*

PHILIP. '. . . final notice . . . steps will be taken . . . distraint . . . proceedings in court . . .'

BELINDA *comes down from the platform to go off after* SELSDON. *She sees* GARRY *and is horrified. She quickly takes the flowers from* BROOKE *and sends her off to fetch* SELSDON.
BELINDA *tries to get the axe away from* GARRY. *He holds it behind his back.*
BELINDA, *still holding the flowers, puts her arms round* GARRY, *trying to reach the axe.*

DOTTY *appears just in time to see* BELINDA *with her arms round* GARRY.

POPPY *urges* BELINDA *upstairs.*

BELINDA *flees up on to the platform to make her entrance. She makes one desperate effort to grab the dress, then enters still carrying the flowers instead.*

BELINDA, *on stage, has to vary the line.*

DOTTY *launches herself upon* GARRY. *He produces the axe in explanation.* DOTTY *snatches it, and raises it to hit* GARRY.

MRS CLACKETT. Oh yes, and that reminds me, a gentleman come about the house.

PHILIP. Don't tell me. I'm not here.

MRS CLACKETT. So I'll just sit down and turn on the . . . sardines, I've forgotten the sardines! I don't know — if it wasn't fixed to my shoulders I'd forget what day it was.

*Exit* MRS CLACKETT *to the service quarters.*

PHILIP. I didn't get this! I'm not here. I'm in Spain. But if I didn't get it I didn't open it.

*Enter* FLAVIA *from the bedroom. She is holding the dress that* VICKI *arrived in.*

FLAVIA. Darling, I never had a dress, or rather bunch of flowers like this, did I?

PHILIP (*abstracted*): Didn't you?

FLAVIA. I shouldn't buy anything as tarty as this . . . Oh, it's not something you gave me, is it?

PHILIP. I should never have touched it.

FLAVIA. No, it's lovely.

PHILIP. Stick it down. Put it back. Never saw it.

*Exit PHILIP into study.*

FREDERICK *appears, and snatches the axe from* DOTTY, *in the nick of time. He innocently gives it to* GARRY, *who raises it to hit* FREDERICK. DOTTY *snatches it from* GARRY, *and raises it to hit him.* BELINDA *appears and snatches the axe from* DOTTY, *as* GARRY *makes his entrance.*

FLAVIA. Well, I'll put it in the attic, with all the other things you gave me that are too precious to wear.

*Exit FLAVIA along the upstairs corridor.*

*Enter* TIM *from the dressing-rooms. He grabs the axe from* BELINDA *and returns to the dressing-rooms.*

*Enter* ROGER *through the front door, still carrying both plates of sardines.*

ROGER. All right, all right . . . Now the study door's open again! What's going on?

*He puts the sardines down — one plate on the telephone table, where it was before, one near the front door — and goes towards the study, but stops at the sound of urgent knocking overhead.*

BELINDA *is going to follow him, but then realises that there is no knocking because* BROOKE *is still off.*

Knocking!

GARRY, *on stage repeats the cue.*
BELINDA *realises what's wrong, and knocks on the set with a prop.*

Knocking . . .! Knocking. . .?

Upstairs!

*Runs upstairs. Knocking.*

Oh my God, there's something in the airing cupboard!

*Only* BROOKE *doesn't
make her entrance, because
she is still off.*

*GARRY comes through
the linen cupboard door
to look for* BROOKE.

*GARRY improvises.*

*Unlocks it and opens it.
Enter* VICKI.

ROGER. Oh, it's you.

Is it you . . .? I mean, you
know, hidden under all the
sheets and towels in here . . .
I can't just stand here and,
you know, indefinitely . . .

*BELINDA tells* POPPY
*to read in* BROOKE's *part
from the book. Then she
hands the flowers to*
FREDERICK *and runs off
to the dressing-rooms, still
holding the axe.*

POPPY (*reads*): Of course
it's me! You put me in
here! In the dark! With all
black sheets and things!

POPPY. Why did *I* lock the
door? Why did *you* lock
the door!

ROGER. But, darling, why
did you lock the door?

ROGER. *I* didn't lock the
door!

*Enter* LLOYD *through the
pass door. He demands
silently to know what's
going on.* FREDERICK *tries
to explain, while* POPPY
*and* GARRY *continue to
play the scene.*

POPPY. *Someone* locked the
door!

ROGER. Anyway, we can't
stand here like this.

FREDERICK *hands*
LLOYD *the flowers to*
*make ready for his*
*entrance.* LLOYD *hurriedly*
*soothes* DOTTY.

POPPY. Like what?

ROGER. In your underwear.

POPPY. OK, I'll take it off.

ROGER. In here, in here!

LLOYD *shoves the flowers*
*into* DOTTY's *hands to get*
*rid of them, and tears*
POPPY's *skirt off, so that*
*she can go on for* BROOKE.

*Exit* ROGER *into the*
*bedroom.*
*Enter* PHILIP *from the*
*study, holding the tax*
*demand, the envelope, and*
*a tube of glue.*

*Enter* BELINDA *from the*
*dressing-rooms, with*
BROOKE. BROOKE *peers*
*at the undressing of*
POPPY.

PHILIP. Darling, this glue.
It's not that special quick-
drying sort, is it, that you
can never get unstuck . . .
Oh, Mrs Clackett's made us
some sardines.

LLOYD *abandons* POPPY,
*and urges* BROOKE *up the*
*stairs for her next scene,*
*for which she is now late.*

*Exit* PHILIP *into the study*
*with the tax demand,*
*envelope, glue, and the*
*plate of sardines from the*
*telephone table.*
*Enter* ROGER *from the*
*bedroom, holding the hot-*
*water bottle. He looks up*
*and down the landing.*

GARRY *comes back through*
*the bedroom door to look*
*for* BROOKE.
*He improvises.*

ROGER. A hot water bottle!
*I* didn't put it there!

I didn't put this hot water
bottle, I mean, you know,
I'm standing out there,
with the hot water bottle
in my hands . . .

BROOKE *makes her
entrance through the linen
cupboard door, and starts
playing the previous scene
that she missed.*

DOTTY *asks LLOYD if
the flowers are really for
her. He pushes them back
to her absently, concerned
about BROOKE onstage.
DOTTY is very touched.
She gives LLOYD a grateful
kiss, just as GARRY
appears to see it.*

VICKI. Of course it's me! You
put me in here! In the dark!
With all black sheets and
things!

ROGER. Someone in the
bathroom, filling hot water
bottles . . . What?

*Exit ROGER into the
mezzanine bathroom.*

VICKI. Why did you lock
the door?

GARRY *moves closer to
see, and cuts three pages
of script.*

*He panics, unable for a
moment to think where he
is, then enters through the
airing-cupboard instead of
the bedroom.
Everyone backstage
panics: 'Where are we?'
POPPY desperately turns
over the pages of the book
to find the new place,
while people look over her
shoulder.
Enter TIM from the
dressing-rooms leading
SELSDON who is holding
his trousers up. TIM is
holding the axe and the
whisky. He hands the
whisky to FREDERICK.*

ROGER. Don't panic! Don't
panic!

*Enter ROGER, and goes
downstairs.*

There's some perfectly
rational explanation for all
this. I'll fetch Mrs Splotchett
and she'll tell us what's
happening. You wait here . . .
You can't stand here
looking like that . . . You
wait in the study . . . Study,
study, study!

*Exit ROGER into the
service quarters.*

FREDERICK, *roars with*
*surprise.*

VICKI *opens the study*
*door. There is a roar of*
*exasperation from* PHILIP,
*off. She turns and flees.*

VICKI. Roger! There's something in there! Where are
you?

FREDERICK *hastily*
*conceals the whisky under*
*the chairs and makes his*
*entrance.*

*There is another cry from*
PHILIP, *off. Exit* VICKI
*blindly through the front*
*door.*
*Enter* PHILIP *from the*
*study. He is holding the*
*tax demand in his right*
*hand, and one of the plates*
*of sardines in his left.*

TIM *gives the axe to*
LLOYD *and takes the*
*flowers from* DOTTY, *who*
*snatches them right back,*
*leaving* TIM *with only one.*
*He hands this to* LLOYD,
*who hands it to* BROOKE.
*She peers at it as it keels*
*sadly over.* LLOYD *gives*
*money to* TIM, *who exits*
*wearily to the dressing-rooms.*

PHILIP. Darling, I know this
is going to sound silly,
but . . .

*He struggles to get the tax*
*demand unstuck from his*
*fingers, encumbered by the*
*plate of sardines.*

*Enter* FLAVIA *along the*
*upstairs corridor, carrying*
*various pieces of bric-a-brac.*

FLAVIA. Darling, if we're not
going to bed I'm going to
clear out the attic.

PHILIP. Darling, I can't come
to bed! I'm glued to a tax
demand!

FLAVIA. Darling, why don't
you put the sardines down?

SELSDON *is explaining to*
*everyone where he was, by*

PHILIP *puts the plate of*
*sardines down on the table.*

*a show of pulling a chain. This demonstration causes his trousers to fall down.*

 

 

 

SELSDON *stoops to retrieve his fallen trousers, and sees the whisky that* FREDERICK *concealed beneath the chairs. He picks it up, and* LLOYD *snatches it out of his hand and gives it to* DOTTY. FREDERICK *repeats the cue, and slams the door again.*

*They all suddenly realise that this is* SELSDON's *cue. They rush him to the window. He raises his arms to open the window and his trousers fall down. They bundle him on as best they can.*

---

*But when he takes his hand away the sardines come with it.*

PHILIP. Darling, I'm stuck to the sardines!

FLAVIA. Darling, don't play the fool. Get that bottle marked poison in the downstairs loo. That eats through anything.

*Exit* FLAVIA *along the upstairs corridor.*

PHILIP (*flaps the tax demand*) I've heard of people getting stuck with a problem, but this is ridiculous.

*Exit* PHILIP *into the downstairs bathroom.*

PHILIP. But this is ridiculous.

*Exit* PHILIP *into the downstairs bathroom.*

 

 

 

 

*The window opens, and through it appears an elderly* BURGLAR. *He has great character, but is in need of extensive repair and modernisation.*

GARRY *snatches the
flowers from* DOTTY. *She
snatches them back.*

LLOYD *parts them with the
axe. He gently takes the
flowers from* DOTTY *and
hands them to* FREDERICK
*while he gives the axe to*
BELINDA.
BELINDA *uses the axe to
keep* DOTTY *and* GARRY
*apart.* FREDERICK *hands
the flowers to* POPPY,
*explaining that they are
from* LLOYD. POPPY,
*touched, takes this as the
cue to come down and say
what she has to say to*
LLOYD. BROOKE
*myopically compares her
miserable flower with*
POPPY'S *full bunch.*
LLOYD, *pursued by*
POPPY, *takes a fortifying
swig of whisky.* POPPY
*watches him. So does*
SELSDON, *as he looks
through the front door.*
He *dries in amaze-
ment.*

SELSDON. Yes? Yes? Line?
Prompt?

POPPY *runs back with the*

BURGLAR. No bars, no
burglar alarm. They ought
to be prosecuted for
incitement.

*He climbs in.*

No, but sometimes it makes
me want to sit down and
weep. When I think I used
to do banks! When I
remember I used to do
bullion vaults! What am I
doing now? — I'm breaking
into paper bags!

*Pours himself a drink.*

I know they're all in Spain,
cause the old turkey in the
kitchen told me so. And I
know *she's* out, cause I've
just seen her come out of the
front door in her swimming
costume . . . Where is the
front door . . .?

*Peers short-sightedly, then
opens the front door ready
for his departure.*

*flowers to the corner to
give him his prompt.*

POPPY. Right, get the van
loaded.

SELSDON. What?

OMNES (*shout*): Get the van
loaded!

SELSDON *runs back on.
BROOKE throws her single
flower back at LLOYD and
goes off to the dressing-
rooms, hurt.*

Right, get the van loaded.
No rush. I've only got
all flaming afternoon!
What are they offering?
(*Peers at the television.*)
One microwave oven.

*Unplugs it and puts it on
the sofa.*

FREDERICK, *realising he
has been tactless, insists
to LLOYD that he will go
after her.*

What? Fifty quid? Hardly
worth lifting it.

*Picks up his drink and
inspects the paintings and
ornaments.*

Junk . . . Junk . . . If you
insist . . .

BELINDA, *with the axe,
escorts DOTTY and
GARRY to make their
entrance.*

*Pockets some small item.*

Where's his desk? No, they
all say the sme thing — it's
hard to adjust to retirement.

BELINDA *takes the
whisky from LLOYD and
holds it up to see how
much has been drunk.
SELSDON takes the whisky
from her.*

*Exit BURGLAR into the
study, holding his drink.*

*Enter ROGER from the
service quarters, followed
by MRS CLACKETT, who
is holding another plate
of sardines.*

ROGER. . . . And the prospective tenant naturally wishes to know if there is any previous history of paranormal phenomena.

LLOYD *tries to get the bottle away from him.*

MRS CLACKETT. Oh, yes, dear, it's all nice and paranormal.

ROGER. I mean, has anything ever dematerialised before? Has anything ever flown about?

SELSDON, *shocked at this open craving, keeps the bottle out of his reach.*

MRS CLACKETT *puts the sardines down on the telephone table, moves the television set back, plugs it in, and closes the front door.*

*Enter* TIM *with a third, very small, bunch of flowers. He gives them to* LLOYD, *very insistent that they are put into his hands directly.*

MRS CLACKETT. Flown about? No, the things move themselves on their own two feet, just like they do in any house.

ROGER. I'll tell the prospective tenant. She is inspecting the study.

LLOYD *hands the flowers to* BELINDA *while he deals with* SELSDON. SELSDON *conceals the whisky in the fire-bucket, while* LLOYD *is distracted by* BELINDA.

*He opens the study door and then closes it again.*

There's a man in there!

MRS CLACKETT. No, no, there's no one in the house, love.

SELSDON *demonstrates that his hands are empty.* LLOYD *searches him.*

ROGER (*opens the study door*): Look! Look! He's . . . searching for something.

BELINDA *hands the axe to* TIM *and gives* LLOYD *a grateful kiss.*
*Enter* FREDERICK *from the dressing-rooms, bringing* BROOKE *back.*
*She peers at the spectacle of* BELINDA, *with flowers, kissing* LLOYD.

TIM, *seeing this, hands the axe to* FREDERICK, *and wearily holds out his hand for money.*
LLOYD *wearily gives him his last small change.*

*Exit* TIM *to the dressing-rooms.* BELINDA *suddenly realises that her flowers are attracting jealous attention, and puts them on* POPPY's *table with the other flowers.*

BROOKE *turns to go back to the dressing-rooms, upset again.*
LLOYD *stops her, and looks round for some token of his affection to give her instead of the flowers.*

MRS CLACKETT (*glances briefly*): I can't see no one.

ROGER. You can't see him? But this is extraordinary! And where is my prospective tenant? I left her in there! She's gone! My prospective tenant has disappeared!

*He closes the study door, and looks round the living room. He sees the sardines on the telephone table.*

Oh my God.

MRS CLACKETT. Now what?

ROGER. There!

MRS CLACKETT. Where?

ROGER. The sardines!

MRS CLACKETT. Oh, the sardines.

ROGER. You can see the sardines, can you?

MRS CLACKETT. I can see the sardines.

ROGER *touches them cautiously, then picks up the plate.*

I can see the way they're going, too.

ROGER. I'm not letting these sardines out of my hand. But where is my prospective tenant?

*He goes upstairs, holding the sardines.*

FREDERICK, *tidily putting the axe back on the firepoint, finds the whisky and holds it aloft — another bottle!*

MRS CLACKETT. I can see I'm going to be opening sardines all night, in and out of here like the cuckoo on a clock.

*Exit* MRS CLACKETT *into the service quarters.*

SELSDON *takes the bottle from* FREDERICK, *but* LLOYD *takes it from* SELSDON *in time for* SELSDON *to make his entrance.*
LLOYD *tries to give the whisky to* BROOKE, *but* FREDERICK *takes it out of his hands to hide it.*

ROGER. Vicki! Vicki!

*Exit* ROGER *into the mezzanine bathroom.*
*Enter* BURGLAR *from the study, carrying an armful of silver cups, etc.*

BURGLAR. He said, 'Charles,' he said. 'You're seventy years old. It's time to hang up the sawn-off shotgun. It's time to let a younger man take over the ammonia bottle.

LLOYD *takes it back.* FREDERICK *takes it away again.*

*Dumps the silverware on the sofa, and exits into the study.*
*Enter* ROGER *from mezzanine bathroom.*

LLOYD *retrieves it.* FREDERICK *takes it, and hides it on the platform.*

ROGER. Where's she gone? She hasn't gone back in the bedroom?

GARRY *makes his exit.*

*Exit* ROGER *into the bedroom.*
*Enter* BURGLAR *from the study, carrying* PHILIP's *box and bag. He empties out the contents*

*of the box behind the sofa, and loads the silverware into it.*

BURGLAR. I said, 'I may be seventy, but I've still got all my wits about me.' He didn't have any answer to that.

*He leans down and tips the plate of sardines he is carrying over* DOTTY's *head, then makes his entrance.*

*Enter* ROGER *from the bedroom, still holding the sardines.*

ROGER (*calls*): Vicki! Vicki

GARRY *makes his exit, picks up the whisky, and takes a swig.*

*Exit* ROGER *into the linen cupboard.*

*While his head is back,* DOTTY *ties his shoelaces together.*

BURGLAR. Or if he did, *I* didn't hear it.

*Exit* BURGLAR *into study, not having seen or heard* ROGER.
*Enter* PHILIP *from the downstairs bathroom. His right hand is still stuck to the tax demand, his left to the plate of sardines.*

PHILIP: Darling, this stuff in the bottle. It *doesn't* eat through glue . . . It just eats through *trousers!* Darling, if it eats through trousers, you don't think it goes on and eats through . . . Listen, darling, I think I'd better get these trousers off! (*He begins to do so, as best he*

LLOYD *tries to warn* GARRY. GARRY *brushes him aside because he has an entrance coming up.*

*can.*) Darling, quick, this is an emergency! Have we got any stuff that stops the stuff that stops the stuff? I mean, if it eats through absolutely anything . . . Darling, I think I can feel it! I think it's eating through . . . absolutely everything!

GARRY *puts the whisky down and makes his entrance, falling over his feet.*

*Enter* ROGER *from the linen cupboard, still holding the sardines.*

ROGER. There's something evil in this house.

PHILIP *pulls up his trousers.*

DOTTY *demonstrates to* BELINDA *and* LLOYD *what she did.*
*They all three try to see what's happening on stage.*

PHILIP (*aside*): The Inland Revenue!

SELSDON *finds the bottle on the platform — yet another bottle!*

ROGER (*frightened*): He's back!

PHILIP. No!

LLOYD *takes it away from him mechanically.*

ROGER. No?

PHILIP. I'm not here.

LLOYD, DOTTY *and* BELINDA *all take swigs from it in turn, absent-mindedly, as they follow events on stage.*

ROGER. Oh my God.

PHILIP. I'm abroad.

ROGER. He's walking abroad.

PHILIP. I must go.

ROGER. Stay!

PHILIP. I'm not staying.

SELSDON *just misses it each time as they pass it absently fom hand to hand.*

ROGER. Speak!

PHILIP. Only in the presence of my lawyer.

ROGER. Only in the . . .?
Hold on. Hold on. You're
just an intruder, an
ordinary intruder!

PHILIP. Well, nice to meet
you.

*Waves goodbye with his
right hand, then sees the
tax demand on it, and
hurriedly puts it away
behind his back.*

I mean, have a sardine.

*Offers the sardines on his
left hand. His trousers,
unsupported, fall down.*

DOTTY *holds up her
hand for silence, and they
all wait for the crash.*

ROGER. No, you're not!
You're a sex criminal! I'm
going to come downstairs
and sort you out.

*The sounds of* GARRY
*falling downstairs on
stage, which even
SELSDON can hear.*

ROGER *comes downstairs.*

PHILIP. Oh, you've got some
sardines. Well, if there's
nothing I can offer you . . .

*No response on stage from
GARRY. They listen, and
as they listen their
laughter dies away.
FREDERICK, on stage,
improvises a line.*

Are you all right?

*No reply.
BELINDA turns to DOTTY
in horror: You've killed
him! BELINDA opens
the study door to go to
GARRY. LLOYD restrains
her.*

*At the sound of* GARRY's *voice, they all relax.*

LLOYD *takes another swig of whisky.*

FREDERICK *makes his exit, trousers round his ankles, handkerchief pressed to his nose.*
BELINDA *hugs him.*
DOTTY *tears him away from her and hugs him.*
BELINDA *tears him back again.* DOTTY *snatches the whisky bottle from* LLOYD *to hit* BELINDA, *but she moves and* DOTTY *hits* BROOKE *instead. She loses her lenses.*

*Everyone is now occupied by this next problem.*
GARRY *repeats the cue.*
BROOKE *is guided to the window for her entrance.*

ROGER (*into the phone*):
Police!

PHILIP. . . . I think I'll be running along.

*Runs, his trousers still round his ankles.*
*Exit through front door.*

ROGER. Come back . . .!
(*Into the phone:*) Hello —
police! Someone has broken into my house! Or rather someone has broken into someone's house . . . Yes, a sex criminal! And a young woman is missing!

*Enter* BROOKE *through the window.*

VICKI. It's in the garden now, and it's a man!

ROGER (*into the phone*): Sorry — the young woman has reappeared. (*Hand over phone.*) Are you all right?

VICKI. No, he almost saw me!

ROGER (*into the phone*): He almost saw her . . . No, but he's a burglar as well! He's taken our things!

VICKI (*finds* PHILIP's *bags*):
The things are here.

ROGER (*into the phone*): The
things have come back. So
we're just missing a plate of
sardines.

SELSDON *suggests to*
DOTTY *that the lenses*
*may be in her clothes.*

VICKI (*finds the sardines left*
*near the front door by*
ROGER): Here are the
sardines.

ROGER (*into the phone*):
And we've found the
sardines.

VICKI. This is the police? You
want the police here — in
my underwear?

ROGER (*into the phone*): So
what am I saying? I'm
saying, let's say no more
about it. (*Puts the phone*
*down.*) I thought something
terrible had happened to
you!

VICKI. It has! I know him!

ROGER. You know him?

POPPY *asks* LLOYD *if*
*this is a good moment for*
*their talk.*
*He waves her away.*

VICKI. He's dealt with by
our office!

ROGER. He's just an ordinary
sex criminal!

SELSDON *searches*
DOTTY's *clothes. She*
*can't understand what*
*he's after.*

VICKI. Yes, but he mustn't
see me like this! You have
to keep up certain standards
if you work for Inland
Revenue!

ROGER. Well, put something on!

VICKI. I haven't got anything!

ROGER. There must be something in the bathroom!

*He picks up the box and bag and leads the way upstairs towards the mezzanine bathroom.*

Bring the sardines!

GARRY *comes raging off, his shoes still tied together. He gazes in amazement at the sight of* DOTTY *and* SELSDON *below.* GARRY *repeats the cue.* LLOYD *rushes* SELSDON *on.*

*Exeunt* ROGER *and* VICKI *into the mezzanine bathroom.*

*Enter the* BURGLAR *from the study, carrying a tape-recorder.*

BURGLAR. 'What?' I said. 'When have I ever needed to run off in the middle of a job to have a Jimmy Riddle?'

*Puts the tape-recorder down by the front door.*

GARRY *starts down the stairs to sort people out, but the state of his shoes prevents his getting more than a step or two before he has to return to make his entrance .*

BURGLAR. 'Except when some stupid berk goes and starts talking about it . . .?' Oh, my Gawd! Where is it?

*Enter* ROGER *from the mezzanine bathroom, carrying the box and bags.*

ROGER. Just stay in there, and don't come out till you've got dressed.

*Enter* VICKI *from the mezzanine bathroom, holding up a very short off-the-shoulder white nightdress.*

FREDERICK *takes over the search in* DOTTY's *clothes.*

GARRY, *gazing furiously down at* FREDERICK *and* DOTTY, *moves to attack* FREDERICK.

*Exit* ROGER *into the bedroom.*

VICKI. But I can't go around in front of our taxpayers wearing *this*!

*Exit* VICKI *into the bedroom.*

BURGLAR. I knew I shouldn't have brought the subject up.

*But* GARRY *is still hobbled, and* FREDERICK *has to make his entrance.*

*Exit* BURGLAR *into the open door of the mezzanine bathroom.*

*Enter* PHILIP *through the front door.*

GARRY *tries to get* BROOKE *to untie him. But she has to make her entrance.*

PHILIP. Darling! Help! Where are you?

*Enter* VICKI *from the bedroom, holding the nightdress, followed by* ROGER.

*Exit* PHILIP *hurriedly into the downstairs bathroom.*

ROGER. Just put it on! It's a start, at any rate! I'll find a bottom — I'll find a top — I'll find something.

TIM *enters from the dressing-rooms, carrying a*

*Exit* ROGER *into the bedroom.*

*cactus, which he gives to*
LLOYD.
GARRY *cries out at the*
*sight of* LLOYD *peering*
*into* DOTTY's *clothing.*
LLOYD *hands the cactus to*
DOTTY, *who absently*
*hands it to* GARRY. LLOYD
*bends over* DOTTY's *clothes*
*again, and* GARRY *rams*
*the cactus up against*
LLOYD's *bottom. Then*
GARRY *hobbles back*
*upstairs, still holding the*
*cactus.* LLOYD *tries to*
*pursue him, but is stopped*
*by the pain.*
GARRY *puts the cactus*
*down on the platform. He*
*takes the ends of the bed-*
*sheets that are hanging up*
*outside the bedroom door,*
*waiting for* FREDERICK
*and* BROOKE, *and ties*
*them together.*

*Exit* VICKI *into the*
*mezzanine bathroom.*
*Enter* VICKI *from the*
*mezzanine bathroom.*

VICKI. Someone in there! It's
him!

*Exit* VICKI *hurriedly into*
*the downstairs bathroom.*
*Enter* FLAVIA *along*
*upstairs corridor, carrying*
*an old biscuit tin.*

FLAVIA. Oh, darling, I'm
finding such lovely things!

*VICKI screams off.*

Do you remember this old
biscuit tin . . .

*Enter* VICKI *from the*
*downstairs bathroom. She*
*stops at the sight of*
FLAVIA.

. . . you gave me on the
very first anniversary of
our . . .? Who are you?

VICKI. Oh my God, it's his
wife and dependents!

*She puts her hands over*
*her face.*

*Enter* PHILIP *from the*
*downstairs bathroom, still*
*with his hands encumbered,*
*holding the nightdress*
*now as well, and keeping*
*his trousers up with his*
*elbows.*

PHILIP. I've taken your dress off you!

*FLAVIA gasps. PHILIP looks up at the gallery and sees her.*

PHILIP (*to* FLAVIA): Where have you been? I've been going mad! Look at the state I'm in!

*He holds up his hands to show FLAVIA the state he is in, and his trousers fall down.*
*The biscuit tin slips from FLAVIA's horrified hands, and crashes on the floor of the living room below. PHILIP hurries towards the stairs, trousers around his ankles, hands extended in supplication.*

*VICKI flees before him and takes refuge in the linen cupboard.*

BROOKE *makes her exit, and* GARRY *points out the*

PHILIP. Darling, I was just trying to explain to her about Inland Revenue being after us, and my fingers got stuck!

*Exit FLAVIA, with a cry of pain, along the upstairs corridor.*

*cactus as he passes her on the way to make his entrance.*

*Enter ROGER from the bedroom, directly in PHILIP's path. PHILIP holds up the nightdress*

BROOKE *comes down from the platform holding the cactus.* DOTTY *pulls*

*a cactus needle out of
LLOYD's bottom.*

*up in front of his face.*

ROGER. Don't keep waving
that thing in my face! I'm
*trying* to find something!
I'll look in the other rooms.

*Exit ROGER along
upstairs corridor.
PHILIP turns to go back
downstairs. The mezzanine
lavatory flushes. He stops.
Enter the BURGLAR from
the mezzanine bathroom,
holding two gold taps.*

BROOKE *stands gazing
in amazement as LLOYD
lowers his trousers and
bends over, while DOTTY
pulls needles out of his
bottom.*
BELINDA *watches the
scene from the platform.
So does GARRY.*
TIM *warns LLOYD that
GARRY is hobbling
downstairs again.*
LLOYD *quickly pulls up
his trousers.*
TIM *takes the cactus from
BROOKE before GARRY
can get it and use it again.*

BURGLAR. One pair gold
taps, anyway . . .

*He stops at the sight of
PHILIP.*

BURGLAR. Oh, my Gawd!

PHILIP. Who are you?

BURGLAR. Me? Fixing the
taps.

PHILIP. Tax? Income tax?

BURGLAR. That's right,
governor. In come the
new taps — out go the old
taps.

*Exit BURGLAR into the
mezzanine bathroom.*

PHILIP. Tax-inspectors
everywhere!

ROGER (*off*): Oh my God!

PHILIP. The other one!

GARRY *has to turn back and go up to the platform again to make his entrance.*

LLOYD *lowers his trousers again for* DOTTY *to resume operations.*

GARRY *makes his exit, and* LLOYD *hurriedly decides that he needs no further attention.*

FREDERICK *makes his exit and picks up the bedsheets which are waiting for him and* BROOKE *to put on. He flaps them at* BROOKE *from the platform to remind her about her change.*

BROOKE *peers at the flapping sheets, and turns to go. But* LLOYD *detains her while he takes the cactus from* TIM *and gives it to her, explaining that*

---

*Exit* PHILIP *into the bedroom, holding the nightdress in front of his face.*
*Enter* ROGER *along the upstairs corridor.*

ROGER. Tin boxes flying about! There *is* something funny going on here! Are you dressed yet?

*Exit* ROGER *into mezzanine bathroom.*
*Enter* PHILIP *from the bedroom, trying to pull the nightdress off his head.*

PHILIP. Darling! I've got it stuck to my head now!

*Enter* ROGER *from the mezzanine bathroom.*

*Exit* PHILIP *into the bedroom.*

ROGER. A man!

*Enter the* BURGLAR *from the mezzanine bathroom.*

BURGLAR. Just doing the taps, governor.

ROGER. Attacks? Not — attacks on women?

BURGLAR. Try anything, governor, but I'll do the taps on the bath first.

*Exit the* BURGLAR *into the mezzanine bathroom.*

ROGER. Sex criminals every-

*it is a token of his
continuing affection. She
peers at it, and he takes
in the nature of the present
for the first time himself.
He turns in pained query
to* TIM, *who gestures
that it was all the shop had
left — all the rest of their
stock is now on* POPPY's
*desk.* FREDERICK *flaps
the sheets in desperation.*
BROOKE *runs up the
steps with the cactus.*

where! Where is Vicki?
Vicki . . .?

*Exit* ROGER *into
downstairs bathroom.
Enter* BURGLAR *from
mezzanine bathroom,
heading for the front door.*

BURGLAR. People everywhere!
I'm off. A tax on women?
I don't know, they'll put
a tax on anything these
days.

*Enter* ROGER *from the
downstairs bathroom.
The* BURGLAR *makes a
U-turn and heads back
towards the mezzanine
bathroom.*

ROGER. If I can't find her,
you're going to be in
trouble, you see.

BURGLAR. W.C.? I'll fix it.

SELSDON *makes his exit.*
BROOKE *pushes the cactus
into* SELSDON's *hands as
she passes.
There is a swirl of sheets
as* FREDERICK *attempts
to dress* BROOKE *in time
for her entrance. They
discover they are tied
together as they attempt to
enter through separate
doors.* BELINDA, *upstairs
for her entrance, goes to try
and disentangle them.*

*Exit* BURGLAR *into
mezzanine bathroom.*

ROGER. Vicki . . .?

*Exit* ROGER *through
the front door.*

SELSDON, *standing
outside the mezzanine
bathroom, joins in. He is
still holding the cactus. He
and the cactus together
make things worse.*

FREDERICK *and* BROOKE
*miss their entrance.* GARRY
*watches with pleasure, until*
LLOYD *tells him to go on
and hold the fort. He
improvises.*

*Enter* ROGER *through the
front door.*

ROGER. No sheikh yet? I
thought he was coming at
four? I mean, it's nearly,
you know, four now . . .
Well, it's after three . . .
Because I've been standing
here for a good, you know,
it seems like forever . . .
What's the time now? It
must be getting on for, you
know . . . it must be getting
on for *five* . . .

SELSDON *gives up and
comes downstairs with the
cactus. He sits on the bottom
step, exhausted, and closes
his eyes.*

FREDERICK *and* BROOKE
*enter through one door
together.*

LLOYD *subsides into a
chair and takes a pill.*

Oh, you're here already,
hiding in the, anyway . . .
And this is your charming
wife? So you want to see
over the house now, do you,
Sheikh? Right. Well. Since
you're upstairs already . . .

ROGER *goes upstairs.*

*Enter* FLAVIA *along the
upstairs corridor, carrying
a vase.*

TIM *puts the sheet on, ready to go on as* PHILIP's *double.*

FLAVIA. Him and his floozie! I'll break this over their heads!

ROGER. . . . let's start downstairs.

ROGER, PHILIP, *and* VICKI *go downstairs.*

FLAVIA. Who are you? Who are these creatures?

ROGER (*to* PHILIP *and* VICKI): I'm sorry about this. I don't know who she is. No connection with the house, I assure you.

DOTTY *points* SELSDON *out to* TIM, *then makes her entrance.* TIM *picks up the whisky and looks at the level. He tells* LLOYD *that* SELSDON *is drunk.*

*Enter* MRS CLACKETT *from the service quarters, with another plate of sardines.* ROGER *advances to introduce her.*

Whereas this good lady with the sardines, on the other hand . . .

LLOYD *says this means that* TIM *will have to go on for* SELSDON.

MRS CLACKETT. No other hands, thank you, not in my sardines, 'cause this time I'm eating them.

ROGER. . . . is fully occupied with her sardines, so perhaps the toilet facilities would be of more interest.

*He ushers* PHILIP *and* VICKI *away from* MRS CLACKETT *towards the mezzanine bathroom.*

*They stand the surprised* SELSDON *up.* TIM *takes the cactus away from him and puts it on*

FLAVIA. Mrs Clackett, who

*the steps.*
*Then they take off his*
*burglar's jacket and hat.*
TIM *puts them on.*
LLOYD *now realises that*
TIM *is still wearing the*
*sheet underneath the jacket.*
*Off jacket, off sheet.* TIM
*now realises that* LLOYD
*will have to go on for him.*
*He persuades* LLOYD *to*
*put on the sheet.*
BELINDA *makes her exit*
*and leans down from the*
*platform to ask what's*
*wrong now.* LLOYD *and*
TIM *explain that* SELSDON
*is drunk.* BELINDA *points*
*out that he has made his*
*entrance, and is even now*
*saying his line.*

are these people?

MRS CLACKETT. Oh, we get
them all the time, love.
They're just Arab sheets.

ROGER. I'm sorry about this.

*He opens the door to*
*the mezzanine bathroom.*

But in here . . .

FLAVIA. *Arab* sheets?

*Exit* FLAVIA *into the*
*bedroom.*
*Enter the* BURGLAR *from*
*the mezzanine bathroom.*

ROGER. In here we have . . .

BURGLAR. Ballcocks,
governor. Your ballcocks
have gone.

ROGER. Oh, we have him.

*Enter* FLAVIA *from the*
*bedroom.*

FLAVIA. They're *Irish* sheets!
Irish linen sheets off my
own bed!

TIM *takes off the burglar's*
*kit.* LLOYD *takes off the*
*double's sheet, and* TIM
*puts it on.*

MRS CLACKETT. Oh, the
thieving devils!

ROGER. In the *study,*
however . . .

MRS CLACKETT. You give
me that sheet, you devil!

*She seizes the nearest sheet,*

*and it comes away in her hand to reveal* VICKI.

DOTTY *varies the line, since the sheet has obviously failed to come off* BROOKE.

Oh, there she stands, and the sheet won't come off her so no one in the world can see her.

GARRY *varies his line, too.*

ROGER. It's you! I mean, I think.

*So does* BELINDA.

FLAVIA. It's her! Isn't it?

FREDERICK *makes his exit — with* BROOKE, *since he is still all of piece with her.*

FLAVIA *comes downstairs menacingly.*
*Exit* PHILIP *discreetly into the study.*

SELSDON *improvises a line.*

BURGLAR. It's my little girl! So far as I could see before she went.

BROOKE *gets back on.*

VICKI. Dad!

FLAVIA *stops.*

TIM *makes his entrance.*

*Enter* PHILIP *from the study in amazement. (He is now played by a double.)*

BURGLAR. Our little Vicki, that ran away from home, I thought I'd never see again!

MRS CLACKETT. Well would you believe it!

VICKI (*to* BURGLAR): What are you doing here like this?

FREDERICK *tries to disentangle himself from the sheets.*

BURGLAR. What are *you* doing here like *that*?

VICKI. Me? I'm taking our files on tax evasion to

Inland Revenue in Basingstoke.

PHILIP *collapses behind the sofa, clutching at his heart, unnoticed by the others.*

FLAVIA (*threateningly*): So where's my other sheet?

LLOYD *helps* FREDERICK *scramble into the robes for his entrance as the* SHEIKH.
LLOYD *picks up the whisky from wherever* TIM *left it. He takes a weary swig, and is just about to sit down on the cactus, when he springs up again guiltily, because* POPPY *is standing in front of him reproachfully. She begins to speak anxiously to him, at first in a completely inaudible whisper.*

*Enter through the front door the most sought-after of all properties on the market today — a* SHEIKH. *He is wearing Arab robes, and bears a strong resemblance to* PHILIP, *since he is played by the same actor.*

SHEIKH. Ah! A house of heavenly peace! I rent it!

OMNES. You!

FLAVIA. Is it?

POPPY. Listen, I've got to talk to you *now*. I'm sorry, I know it's not a good moment — it's never a good moment. I keep trying to phone you, but you're never there. I know you're in rehearsals all day, but you're not there at night, either, you're not there in the morning — I don't know *where* you are.

SHEIKH (*with dignity*): Is me? Certainly is me! Who else?

*They all fall upon him.*

ROGER. You walk in asking to view a house like this, when you're nothing but a trouserless tramp! (*He pulls up the* SHEIKH's *robes.*)

LLOYD *gestures that he can't hear, and offers her a*

SHEIKH. What?

*soothing sip of whisky. She brushes it aside, becoming more and more agitated.*

POPPY (*voicing the words, which are still drowned by the dialogue on stage*): No, no, no, I'm not going to be put off, I'm going to tell you, because as soon as that curtain's down you'll be round seeing her, I know that. Well, she's being difficult, isn't she — I saw you with that cactus — I'm not blind. And then you'll be on the next train back to London. I'm afraid I'm starting to know the way you operate, you see, Lloyd — and I bet there's someone else, in Richard III, isn't there, but you can't just walk away from it this time!

LLOYD *wearily, smilingly, soothingly gestures that he can't hear a word.*

POPPY (*out loud*): Well, I'm sorry, but you've *got* to hear, because I'm *pregnant!*

*A gasp from everyone on stage. They both become aware that the act has ended.*

FLAVIA. You toss me aside like a broken china doll! (*She hits him.*)

SHEIKH. What? What?

MRS CLACKETT. You take all the clean sheets! (*Tries to pull the robes off him.*)

VICKI. You snatch my night-dress! (*Tries to pull his burnous off him.*)

SHEIKH. What? What? What?

BURGLAR. And what you're up to with my little girl down there in Basingstoke I won't ask. But I'll tell you one thing, Vicki.

VICKI. What's that, Dad?

BURGLAR. When all around is strife and uncertainty, there's nothing like . . .

*He takes* MRS CLACKETT's *plate.*

BURGLAR. . . . . a good old-fashioned plate of sardines!

LLOYD (*whispers*): And
*curtain!*

POPPY *runs back to the
corner.*

LLOYD *subsides, defeated,
on to the cactus.*

**Curtain.**

*Curtain.*

**ACT ONE**

*The living-room of the Brents' country home. Wednesday
afternoon. (Municipal Theatre, Stockton-on-Tees, Saturday
April 6.)*

*This time the act is being seen from the front again, exactly as
it was the first time, at the rehearsal in Weston-super-Mare. Before
the curtain rises we hear the last of the front-of-house calls.*

POPPY (*over the Tannoy*): Ladies and gentlemen, will you please
take your seats. The performance is about to . . . oh.

*She stops because the curtain has risen to reveal* TIM *checking
the props on stage. The curtain hovers uncertainly, then
descends. When it rises again, the stage is empty and the
telephone is ringing.*

*Enter from the service quarters* MRS CLACKETT, *pursued by*
BELINDA's *foot. She is carrying an imposing plate of sardines,
and she is limping painfully.*

MRS CLACKETT. It's no good you going on. I can't pick sardines
off the floor *and* answer the phone. I've only got one leg.
(*Into phone*:) Hello . . . Yes, but there's no one here, love . . .
No, Mr Brent's not here . . . He lives here, yes, but he don't
live here now because he lives in Spain . . .

*She tries to examine her knee as she talks.*

Mr Philip Brent, that's right . . . The one that writes the plays,
only why he wants to get mixed up in plays God only knows,
he'd be safer off in the lion's cage at the zoo . . . No, she's
in Spain, too, they're all in Spain, there's no one here . . . Am
I in Spain? No, I'm not in Spain, dear, I'm in agony. That's
where I am. One moment I'm standing there with a plate of
sardines, next moment she's kicked me on the kneecap and
there's sardines all over the floor.

*The plate tips as she rubs her knee, and the sardines slide unnoticed on to the floor.*

Here we are, we haven't been going three months, and already she's lashing out with her feet, and here am I, I don't know where I am, I'm eating sardines off the floor with one knee, don't tell us they've gone again . . .

*She looks round for the sardines.*

. . . and if you want anything else you'll have to ring the house-agents, because they've got their hands free to see what they're doing . . . No, they're not in Spain, they're next to the phone in the study. Squire, Squire, Hackham, and hold on, I'm going to do something wrong here, I can't think with one hand.

*She shuffles phone, plate, and newspaper uncertainly.*

Always the same, isn't it. One minute you've got too much on your plate, and next thing you know you've put your foot in it.

*She puts her foot in it.*

Oh, speak of the devil. (*Wipes her shoe on the newspaper.*) They'll all want to go putting their foot in it now, won't they. (*Drops the newspaper over the sardines.*) I'll put that there, look. That'll keep them out of harm's way. But what I'm holding now I *don't* know . . . And off at last I go.

*Exit into the study, holding the empty plate and the telephone receiver. The body of the phone falls off its table and follows halfway to the door. The sound of a key in the lock. The front door opens. On the doorstep stands* ROGER, *carrying a cardboard box.*

ROGER. . . . My housekeeper, yes, but this is her afternoon off.

*The body of the phone begins to creep inconspicuously towards the door.*
*Enter* VICKI.

So we've got the place entirely to ourselves.

ROGER *goes back and brings in a flight bag and closes the front door.*

I'll just check.

*He halts the telephone with a casually placed foot. VICKI gazes round.*

Hello? Anyone at home? No, there's no one here.

*He picks the phone up, and puts it back on its table.*

So what do you think?

*He takes his hand off the phone, and it springs back on to the floor.*

VICKI. Great. And this is all yours?

*The phone starts to creep away again. ROGER casually picks it up as he talks and puts it down on the sideboard.*

ROGER. Just a little shack in the woods, really. Converted posset mill. Sixteenth-century.

VICKI. It must have cost a bomb.

*Another jerk on the wire catapults the phone across the room. VICKI pays no attention to it.*

ROGER. Well, one has to have somewhere to entertain one's business associates. Someone on the phone now, by the look of it.

*He picks the phone up and puts it back on the sideboard.*

It's probably this, you know, this Arab saying he wants to come at four, so I mean I'll just have a word with him and . . .

*He tries to pick up the receiver and finds that it's not there. As the conversation continues he follows the receiver cord along with his hand.*

VICKI. Right, and I've got to get those files to our Basingstoke office by four.

ROGER. Yes, we'll only just manage to pick it in. I mean, we'll only just fit it up. I mean . . .

VICKI. Right, then.

ROGER. We won't bother to pull the champagne.

*He pulls gently at the cord.*

VICKI. All these doors.

ROGER. Oh, only a handful, really. Study. Kitchens, and a self-contained service flat for the . . .

*He tugs hard, and the cord comes away without the receiver.*

. . . receiver.

VICKI. Terrific. And which one's the . . .?

ROGER. What?

VICKI. You know . . .

ROGER. Oh. Through here.

*He bundles up the phone and cable, repeating the line. Opens the downstairs bathroom for her.*

VICKI. Fantastic.

*Exit* VICKI *into the bathroom.* ROGER *tosses the phone casually off after her.*
*Enter* MRS CLACKETT *from the study, still walking with difficulty, and holding the now cordless receiver and a small shovel.*

MRS CLACKETT. I've just come for my sardines.

*Mutual surprise.* ROGER *closes the door to the bathroom.*

ROGER. I'm sorry. I thought there was no one here.

MRS CLACKETT. I'm not here. (*Looks round for the phone, so that she can replace the receiver.*) I don't know *where* I am.

ROGER. I'm from the agents.

MRS CLACKETT. Lost the phone now.

ROGER. Squire, Squire, Hackham, and Dudley.

MRS CLACKETT. Never lost a phone before.

ROGER. I'm Tramplemain.

MRS CLACKETT. I'll just put it up here, look, if anyone wants it.

*She puts the receiver in some handy prominent place.*

ROGER. Oh, right, thanks. No, I just dropped in to . . . go into a few things. Well, to check some of the measurements. Do one or two odd jobs.

*The bathroom door opens. ROGER closes it. MRS CLACKETT looks under the newspaper, then turns round to look for the plate.*

MRS CLACKETT. Now the plate's gone.

ROGER. Oh, and a client. I'm showing a prospective client over the house.

VICKI (*off, opening the door*): What's wrong with this door?

ROGER. She's thinking of renting it. Her interest is definitely aroused.

*Enter VICKI from the bathroom.*
*ROGER steps on to the newspaper.*

VICKI. That's not the bedroom.

ROGER. The bedroom? No, that's the downstairs bathroom and WC suite. And this is the housekeeper. Mrs Crockett.

MRS CLACKETT. Sardines, dear, sardines.

VICKI. Oh. Hi.

ROGER. She's not really here.

MRS CLACKETT. Only you're standing on them.

ROGER (*moves*): It's the royal, you know.

MRS CLACKETT (*looks under the newspaper*): Oh, you shouldn't have stood on them.

ROGER (*to MRS CLACKETT*): Don't worry about us.

MRS CLACKETT. Only I need these sardines, you see.

ROGER. We'll just inspect the house.

MRS CLACKETT. I'll have to give the floor a wash now.

*Exit MRS CLACKETT into study leaving the sardines beneath the newspaper on the floor.*

ROGER. I'm sorry about this.

VICKI. That's all right. We don't want the television, do we?

ROGER. Television? That's right, television, she didn't explain about wanting to watch this royal, you know, because obviously there's been this thing with the . . . (*Indicates the sardines.*) I mean, I'm just, you know, in case anyone's looking at all this and thinking, 'My God!'.

VICKI. Great. Come on, then. (*Starts upstairs.*) I've got to be in Basingstoke by four.

ROGER. Sorry, love. I thought we ought to get that straight.

VICKI. We'll take it up with us.

ROGER. Where are we?

VICKI. And don't let my files out of sight.

ROGER. Hold on. We've got out of . . .

VICKI. What?

ROGER. What?

VICKI. Her?

ROGER. Her? OK — 'her'. Right, because she has been in the family for generations.

*Enter* MRS CLACKETT *from the study, carrying a bottle of whisky.*

MRS CLACKETT. Sardines . . . sardines . . . I'll just give the floor a wash with this, look, and they'll be out of your way. (*Finds the bottle in her hands.*) Look what I've got hold of now!

VICKI. Oh. Great.

MRS CLACKETT. It's like a battlefield out there.

VICKI. Terrific.

MRS CLACKETT *puts the bottle of whisky with the other bottles on the sideboard.*

MRS CLACKETT. I'll put it here, look, then if he wants it he won't know where to find it. Sardines, sardines, You'll have to do the sardines, then, 'cause I've got to go back to the kitchen now and do some more sardines.

*Exit* MRS CLACKETT *to service quarters.*

VICKI. You see? She thinks it's great. She's even making us sardines!

ROGER. OK, so what do you think?

VICKI. I think she's terrific.

ROGER. No, I mean, do you want to do the . . . ? (*Indicates the sardines.*)

VICKI. So which way?

ROGER. I don't know. Kind of parcel them up in the, you know.

VICKI. Up here?

ROGER. I mean, I've got to do the . . . (*Indicates the bag and box.*)

VICKI. In here?

ROGER. OK, you take the . . . (*Bag and box.*) I'll do the . . . (*Sardines.*)

*Exit* VICKI *into mezzanine bathroom, still unable to deviate by a hair's breadth from the script.* ROGER *parcels up the sardines in the newspaper as best he can.*

VICKI. It's another bathroom.

*She reappears.*

ROGER. Box! Bag!

VICKI. Always trying to get me into bathrooms.

ROGER. Bag! Box!

VICKI. This is the airing cupboard.

ROGER. Box! Box! Bag! Bag!

VICKI. Oh, you're in a real state!

ROGER. If we haven't got the, you know, upstairs, I mean, my God!

*ROGER runs to the foot of the stairs, then runs back and puts the parcel of sardines on the telephone table, and picks up the bag and box.*

VICKI. You can't even get the door open.

*Exit* VICKI *into bedroom.*

*The sound of a key in the lock. The door opens, and on the doorstep stands* PHILIP, *carrying a cardboard box.*

PHILIP. Yes, but this is Mrs Clackett's afternoon off.

ROGER *abandons the sardines and flees upstairs with the bag and the box. He finds the bedroom door shut in his face. Enter* FLAVIA.

We've got the place entirely to ourselves.

*Exit* ROGER *into the bedroom with the bag and box.* PHILIP *brings in the flight bag.*

FLAVIA. Look at it!

PHILIP. Do you like it?

FLAVIA. I can't believe it!

PHILIP. The perfect place for an assignation.

FLAVIA. Home.

PHILIP. Home.

FLAVIA (*produces the remains of the phone*): But how odd to find the telephone in the garden!

PHILIP. I'll put it back.

*She hands him the phone — now in a very deteriorated condition — and he attempts to replace it on the telephone table. But it is still connected to its lead, which is too short, since it runs out through the downstairs bathroom door, and back in through the front door.*

FLAVIA. I thought I'd better bring it in.

PHILIP. Very sensible.

*He tugs discreetly at the lead.*

FLAVIA. Someone's bound to want it.

PHILIP. Oh dear. (*Tugs.*)

FLAVIA. Why don't you put it back on the table?

PHILIP. The wire seems to be caught.

FLAVIA. Oh, look, it's caught round the downstairs bathroom.

PHILIP. So it is.

*FLAVIA turns and with discreet violence pulls the lead out of the junction-box where it originates.* PHILIP, *meanwhile, takes the phone back out of the front door, and re-emerges with it through the downstairs bathroom.*

FLAVIA. I think I've disentangled it.

PHILIP. I climbed through the bathroom window and . . . oh . . . oh . . .

*He takes the parcel of sardines off the telephone table and puts the telephone in its place.*

FLAVIA. Anyway, our little secret hideaway.

PHILIP. The last place on earth anyone will . . .

*Attempting to fold up the newspaper briskly and tidily, he becomes distracted by the contents that come oozing out over his hands.*

FLAVIA. . . . look for us, yes, but it's rather funny, creeping in like this.

*Pause.*

PHILIP. Sorry?

FLAVIA. I know what you're thinking. You're thinking, 'It's damned serious!'

PHILIP. Sorry. Yes. It's damned serious!

FLAVIA. You're thinking about Inland Revenue.

PHILIP. Absolutely. Inland Revenue. Well, to cut a long story short, I think I'm going to have a wash and go to bed.

*He puts down the parcel of sardines on the sofa, picks up the bag and box, and starts upstairs.*

FLAVIA (*hurriedly*): Yes, but Inland Revenue! We must have our little talk first about Inland Revenue! Because you're thinking something like, 'If Inland Revenue finds out we're in the country, even for one night, bang goes our claim to be resident abroad, bang goes most of this year's . . . Leave those!

PHILIP *drops the bag and box, but by this time he is already upstairs.*

Downstairs!

PHILIP. Sh!

FLAVIA. Not upstairs!

PHILIP. Inland Revenue may hear us! What?

*Enter* MRS CLACKETT *from the service quarters carrying a fresh plate of sardines.*

MRS CLACKETT (*to herself*): One moment they're kicking you to death, next moment they expect you to come waltzing in with more sardines.

*She puts down the plate of sardines, and goes to sit on the sofa, on the parcel of sardines left there by* PHILIP.

PHILIP (*urgently, looking down from the gallery*): Mrs *Newspaper*!

MRS CLACKETT *jumps up just in time.*

MRS CLACKETT. Oh, you give me a turn! My heart jumped right out of the sofa!

PHILIP. So did mine!

FLAVIA. We thought you'd gone!

MRS CLACKETT (*finds the parcel of sardines and examines it*): I thought you was in Sardinia!

PHILIP. We are! We are!

FLAVIA. You haven't seen us!

PHILIP. We're not here!

MRS CLACKETT. Oh, look, and they've brought me a present home!

FLAVIA. Yes, but the main thing is that the income tax people are after us.

MRS CLACKETT. I can guess which one of them thought of this.

FLAVIA. We're not here. You haven't seen us.

MRS CLACKETT. Lovely helping of mashed sardines.

FLAVIA. Anyway, if anybody asks for us, you don't know nothing. Anything.

MRS CLACKETT. She just leaves them quietly on the sofa.

FLAVIA. So we're off to bed.

MRS CLACKETT. And goes off without waiting to be thanked.

FLAVIA. Has the bed been aired?

MRS CLACKETT. Well, I've got a little surprise for *you*, love. (*Pursues her upstairs.*)

FLAVIA. No? I'll get a hot water bottle.

*Exit* FLAVIA *into the mezzanine bathroom.*

MRS CLACKETT. I'll give you sardines, my sweetheart.

*MRS CLACKETT runs back downstairs and exits into the study with the parcel of sardines.*

PHILIP. Oh . . .

*Enter* FLAVIA *hurriedly from the mezzanine bathroom.*

FLAVIA. So now she's left you all on your own, has she?

PHILIP. Well . . .

FLAVIA. What are you supposed to do? Talk to yourself?

PHILIP. Oh dear.

FLAVIA. Has she told you what she's done with your letters?

*Enter* MRS CLACKETT *from the study, still holding the parcel of sardines.*

MRS CLACKETT. What's she telling you now, love?

FLAVIA (*to* MRS CLACKETT): You haven't told him about his letters! (*To* PHILIP:) She's put them all in the study! All the letters from the income tax!

PHILIP. Oh dear.

MRS CLACKETT. Telling him where his letters are! You don't own him, you know!

*She advances on* FLAVIA *with the parcel of sardines.*

FLAVIA (*retreating*): She's put them all in the little pigeonhouse!

*Exit* FLAVIA *into the mezzanine bathroom.*

PHILIP. In the pigeonhouse?

MRS CLACKETT. Pigeonhole, dear. You come with me. Anybody would think she was married to you.

MRS CLACKETT *leads* PHILIP *firmly off into the study, still carrying the parcel of sardines.* PHILIP's *bag and box are left outside the bedroom door.*
*Enter* ROGER *from the bedroom, still dressed, but with no tie on.*

ROGER. Yes, but I could hear voices!

*He falls over* PHILIP's *bag and box.*
*Enter* VICKI *from the bedroom in her underwear.*

VICKI. Voices? What sort of voices?

ROGER. Box voices. I mean, *people's* boxes.

VICKI. But there's no one here.

ROGER. Darling, I saw the door-handle move! And these bags — I'm not sure they were, you know, when we went into the, do you know what I mean?

VICKI. I still don't see why you've got to put your tie on to look.

ROGER (*picks up the bag and box*): Because if someone left these things outside the, I mean, come *on,* they obviously want them downstairs inside the, you know.

VICKI. Mrs Clockett?

ROGER. It could be. Coming up here on her way to, well, carrying various, I mean, who knows?

VICKI (*looks over the bannisters*): Oh look, she's opened our sardines.

*She moves to go downstairs.* ROGER *puts down the bag and box outside the linen cupboard door and grabs her.*

ROGER. Come back!

VICKI. What?

ROGER. I'll fetch them! You can't go downstairs like that.

VICKI. Why not?

ROGER. Mrs Crackett.

VICKI. Mrs Crackett?

ROGER. She's irreplaceable.

*Enter* MRS CLACKETT *from the study, without the parcel of sardines, wiping her hands.*

MRS CLACKETT (*to herself*): At least I've thanked her properly for the sardines.

ROGER *tries to pull open the linen cupboard door to conceal* VICKI, *but it is obstructed by the bag and box.*

Oh, you're still poking around, are you?

ROGER. Yes, still poking, well, still pulling.

*He tugs at the door again, unaware of the obstruction, and the handle comes off.*

MRS CLACKETT. Good job I can't see far with this leg.

ROGER *moves the bag and box, gets the door of the linen cupboard open one way or another and* VICKI *inside, and rebalances the handle in place.*

ROGER. Just, you know, trying all the doors and I mean checking all the door-handles.

*He starts downstairs, carrying* PHILIP's *bag and box.*

Mrs Blackett . . .

MRS CLACKETT. Clackett, dear, Clackett.

ROGER. Mrs Clackett. Is there anyone else in the house, Mrs Clackett?

MRS CLACKETT. I haven't seen no one, dear.

ROGER. I thought I heard a box. I mean, I found these voices.

MRS CLACKETT. Voices? There's no voices here, love.

ROGER. I must have imagined it.

PHILIP (*off*): Oh my God!

*The sound of a body falling, off, followed by a wailing groan from* PHILIP.

ROGER. I beg your pardon?

MRS CLACKETT (*mimics* PHILIP): Oh my God! (*She crashes things about on the sideboard in imitation of the offstage crash, and ends the performance with a wailing groan.*)

ROGER. Why, what is it?

MRS CLACKETT. The study door's open.

*She crosses and closes it.*

ROGER. They're going to want these inside the . . . (*Indicates the study.*) So I'll put them outside the . . . (*Indicates the front door.*) Then they can, do you know what I mean?

*Exit ROGER through the front door, carrying the bag and box. Enter FLAVIA from the mezzanine bathroom, carrying a first-aid box. She sees the linen cupboard door swinging open as she passes, and pushes it shut, so that the latch closes. The handle comes off in her hand.*

FLAVIA. Nothing but flapping doors in this handle.

*Exit FLAVIA into the bedroom, holding the first-aid box and the handle.*
*Enter from the study PHILIP, holding a tax demand and its envelope. The part is now being played not by FREDERICK but by TIM.*

PHILIP. '. . . final notice . . . steps will be taken . . . distraint . . . proceedings in court . . .'

MRS CLACKETT. Oh my Lord, who are you?

PHILIP. I'm Philip.

MRS CLACKETT. You're Philip? What's happened to *you*?

PHILIP. Well, there were these sardines on the floor . . .

MRS CLACKETT. And he stepped in it!

PHILIP. And I slipped . . .

MRS CLACKETT. She's killed him! She's killed you!

PHILIP. No. He's just a bit shaken. I'll be all right in a minute.

*Exit MRS CLACKETT to the study.*

You weren't going to tell me a gentleman had come about the house, were you?

MRS CLACKETT (*off*): What?

PHILIP. You weren't going to tell me a gentleman had come about the house?

*Enter MRS CLACKETT from the study.*

MRS CLACKETT. That's right. A gentleman come about the house.

PHILIP. Don't tell me. I'm not here.

MRS CLACKETT. You haven't done himself an injury, then?

PHILIP. Leave everything to Squire, Squire, Hackham, and Dudley.

MRS CLACKETT. All right, love. Oh, and he's put your box out in the garden for you.

PHILIP. Let them do anything. Just so long as you don't tell anyone we're here.

MRS CLACKETT. So I'll just sit down and turn on the . . . sardines, I've forgotten the sardines! (*Finds the sardines on the table, where they should be.*) Oh, no, I haven't, I've remembered the sardines! What a surprise! I must go out to the kitchen and make another plate of sardines to celebrate.

*Exit MRS CLACKETT to the service quarters.*

PHILIP. I didn't get this! I'm not here. I'm in Spain. But if I didn't get it I didn't open it.

*Enter FLAVIA from the bedroom. She is holding the dress that VICKI arrived in, and the handle of the linen cupboard.*

FLAVIA. Darling . . . (*She stares at TIM in surprise, then recovers herself and looks at the dress.*) I never had a handle like this, did I?

PHILIP (*abstracted*): Didn't you?

FLAVIA. I shouldn't buy anything as brassy as this . . .

*FLAVIA drops the dress and attempts to replace the handle on the linen cupboard behind her back.*

Oh, it's not something you gave me, is it?

PHILIP. I should never have touched it.

FLAVIA. No, it's lovely.

PHILIP. Stick it down. Put it back. Never saw it.

*Exit* PHILIP *into study.*

FLAVIA. Well, I'll put it in the attic, if anyone else wants to
have a try.

*Exit* FLAVIA *along the upstairs corridor, taking the handle
but leaving the dress on the floor.*
*Enter* ROGER *through the front door, without the bag
and box.*

ROGER. All right, all right . . . Now the study door's open
again! What's going on?

*He goes towards the study, but stops at the sound of urgent
knocking overhead.*

Knocking! (*Knocking.*) Upstairs!

*Runs upstairs. Knocking.*

Oh my God, there's something in the . . . (*Discovers the lack
of a handle.*) Oh my God! (*Knocking.*) Listen! I can't, because
the handle seems to have, you know. You'll just have to . . .

*He demonstrates pushing. Knocking.*

Come on! Come on!

*Knocking.*

I mean, whatever it is in there. Can you hear me? Darling!

*Knocking.*

Look, don't just keep banging! There's nothing I can, I mean
it won't, there's nowhere to . . .

*Knocking. He opens the bedroom door.*

Listen! Climb round into the . . . (*Indicates the bedroom.*)
Squeeze through the, you know, and shin down the, I mean,
there must be some way!

*Knocking.*

ROGER. Oh, for God's sake!

*Exit* ROGER *into the bedroom.*
*Enter* PHILIP *from the study, holding a tax demand and an envelope. He is now being played by* FREDERICK, *with a plaster on his forehead and another bloodstained plaster over his nose.*

PHILIP. '. . . final notice . . . steps will be taken . . . distraint . . . proceedings in court . . .

*Enter* ROGER *from the bedroom, pulling* VICKI *after him.*
PHILIP *gazes at them, baffled.*

ROGER. Oh, it's you.

VICKI. Of course it's me! You put me in here! In the dark with all black sheets and things.

ROGER. I put you in *there*, but you managed to squeeze through the, you know.

VICKI. Why did *I* lock the door? Why did *you* lock the door!

ROGER. I couldn't, I mean, look, look, it's come off!

VICKI. *Someone* locked the door!

PHILIP. Sorry.

*Exit* PHILIP *apologetically into study.*

ROGER. Anyway, we can't stand here like this.

VICKI. Like what?

ROGER. I mean, you know, with people going in and out.

VICKI. OK, I'll take it off.

ROGER. In here, in here!

*Ushers her into the bedroom.*
*Enter* PHILIP *cautiously from the study, holding the tax demand and the envelope.*

PHILIP. '. . . final notice . . . steps will be taken . . . distraint . . . proceedings in court . . .'

*Enter* ROGER *from the bedroom, holding the first aid box.*
*He looks up and down the landing.*
*Enter* VICKI *from the bedroom.*
PHILIP *stares at them.*

VICKI. Now what?

ROGER. A hot water box! *I* didn't put it there!

VICKI. *I* didn't put it there.

PHILIP. Sorry.

*Exit* PHILIP *into the study.*

ROGER. Someone in the bathroom, filling first aid bottles.

*Exit* ROGER *into the mezzanine bathroom.*

VICKI (*anxious*): You don't think there's something creepy going on?

*Exit* VICKI *into mezzanine bathroom.*
*Enter* FLAVIA *along the upstairs corridor.*

FLAVIA. Darling . . . Darling?

*Enter* PHILIP *cautiously from the study. He raises the income tax demand to speak.*

Darling, are you coming to bed or aren't you?

*Exit* FLAVIA *into bedroom.*
*Enter* ROGER *and* VICKI *from the mezzanine bathroom.*
PHILIP *raises his income tax demand to speak.*

ROGER. What did you say?

VICKI. I didn't say anything.

*Exit* PHILIP *into the study.*

ROGER. I mean, there's the door handle. Now there's the first water box.

VICKI. I can feel goose-pimples all over.

ROGER. Yes, quick, get something round you.

VICKI. Get the covers over our heads.

ROGER *is about to open the bedroom door.*

ROGER. Just a moment. What did I do with those sardines?

*He goes downstairs.* VICKI *makes to follow.*

You — wait here.

VICKI (*uneasy*): You hear all sorts of funny things about these old houses.

ROGER. Yes, but this one has been extensively modernised throughout. I can't see how anything creepy would survive oil-fired central heating and . . .

VICKI. What? What is it?

ROGER *stares round in silence.*

What's happening?

ROGER. The sardines. They've gone. (*Sees them.*) No, they haven't. They're here. Oh. Well. My God — I mean — my God!

*He turns and starts back upstairs.* FLAVIA *crawls through the front door. She picks up the sardines and takes them back to the front door.*

You put a plate of sardines down for two minutes, and the last thing you expect to find, I mean, these days, the one thing you don't expect to find when you come back is a plate of, I mean that's *really* weird!

VICKI. Perhaps there is something funny going on. I'm going to get into bed and put my head under the . . .

*She freezes at the sight of the empty table outside the bedroom door.*

ROGER. Because, I mean, there they are! Exactly where I . . .

*He realises that the sardines are not there.*

VICKI. Bag . . .

ROGER *goes back downstairs to investigate.* VICKI *runs after him.* FLAVIA *reacts to the mention of the bag.*

ROGER. I suppose Mrs Sprockett must have, I mean, Jesus, what *is* going on?

*As* ROGER *turns away towards* VICKI, FLAVIA *crawls hurriedly back in, puts the sardines on the table.*

VICKI. Bag!

*Reminded about the bag,* FLAVIA *exits hurriedly through the front door.*

ROGER. Bag?

VICKI. Bag! Bag!

*She drags* ROGER *back upstairs.*

ROGER. What do you mean, bag, bag?

VICKI. Bag! Bag! Bag!

ROGER *looks over the bannisters and sees the sardines.*

ROGER. Sardines!

VICKI. Bag! Bag! Bag!

ROGER. Sardines! Sardines!

VICKI. Bag! Bag! Bag!

*While* ROGER *is gazing at the sardines, and* VICKI *is looking at* ROGER, *the bedroom door opens, and* FLAVIA *puts the flight bag on the table outside.*

ROGER (*tearing himself away from the sight of the sardines*): Bag? What bag?

VICKI (*gazing at the bag*): No bag!

ROGER. No bag?

VICKI. Your bag! Suddenly! Here! Now — gone!

ROGER. It's in the bedroom. (*Sees the bag.*) It *was* in the bedroom. I put it in the bedroom. I'll put it back in the bedroom.

*As* ROGER *goes to open the bedroom door it opens in front of him, and* FLAVIA *begins to come out carrying the box.*

VICKI. Don't go in there!

ROGER *grabs the box and closes the door.*

ROGER. The box!

VICKI. The box?

ROGER. They've *both* not gone!

VICKI. Oh! My files!

ROGER. What on earth is happening? Where's Mrs Spratchett?

*He starts downstairs with the bag and box.* VICKI *follows him.*

You wait in the bedroom.

VICKI. No! No! No!

*She runs downstairs.*

ROGER. Well, get dressed, then!

VICKI. I'm not going in there!

ROGER. I'll fetch your dress out here.

*He puts the bag and box down at the head of stairs, returns
to the bedroom, and sees the dress on the floor.
Exit ROGER into the bedroom.
Enter ROGER from the bedroom.*

Your dress has gone.

*As he speaks he slides the dress over the edge of the gallery with
his foot to get rid of it. It falls on top of VICKI beneath.*

VICKI (*struggling beneath it*): Oh!

ROGER. Don't panic! Don't panic! There's some perfectly
rational explanation for all this . . .

*He starts downstairs, looking over the bannister appalled at
the sight of VICKI below, and falls headlong over the bag
and box at the top of the stairs.
Exit VICKI blindly through the front door with the dress.
Enter PHILIP from the study, still played by FREDERICK.
He is holding a tax demand in his right hand, and one of the
plates of sardines in his left.*

PHILIP. Darling, I know this is going to sound silly, but . . .

*His struggles to get the tax demand unstuck from his fingers,
die away at the sight of ROGER, lying at the bottom of the
stairs.
Enter FLAVIA along the upstairs corridor, carrying further
pieces of bric-a-brac.*

FLAVIA. Darling, if we're not going to bed I'm going to clear
out the attic . . .

PHILIP (*To* ROGER): Are you all right?

FLAVIA. Oh my God!

*She rushes downstairs.*

PHILIP. What happened?

FLAVIA. Can you speak, love?

*Enter MRS CLACKETT in alarm from the service quarters, holding another plate of sardines.*

MRS CLACKETT. Oh, she's killed this one now!

FLAVIA. He's stunned, that's all. Keep going.

PHILIP. Oh dear.

MRS CLACKETT. She's putting sardines on the stairs for them.

FLAVIA. Are you all right, my precious?

ROGER (*lifts his head*): Don't panic! Don't panic!

FLAVIA. He's all right!

PHILIP. Well done.

MRS CLACKETT. She'll get you next time.

FLAVIA. Just keep going.

ROGER. There's some perfectly rational explanation for all this.

PHILIP. Where are we?

ROGER. I'll fetch Mrs Splotchett and she'll tell us what's happening. . .

MRS CLACKETT. You've fetched her. I'm here.

ROGER. I've fetched Mrs Splotchett and she'll tell us what's happening.

MRS CLACKETT. She won't, you know. She doesn't know whether it's Christmas or whether it's Clacton.

PHILIP. Oh dear.

FLAVIA. *I'll* tell you what's happening.

ROGER. There's a man in there! Yes?

FLAVIA. He's not in there, my precious — he's in here, look, and so am I.

MRS CLACKETT. No, no, there's no one in the house, love. Yes?

FLAVIA. No, look, I know this is a great surprise for everyone. I mean, it's quite a shock for *us*, finding a man lying at the bottom of the stairs! (*To* PHILIP:) Isn't it, darling?

PHILIP. Oh dear.

FLAVIA. But now we've all met we'll just have to — well, we'll just have to introduce ourselves! Won't we, darling?

PHILIP. Oh dear. Oh dear.

FLAVIA. This is my husband. I'm afraid he hates surprises! So, darling, why don't you go off and get that bottle marked poison in the downstairs loo? That eats through anything.

PHILIP. Eats through anything. Right. Thank you. Thank you. Yes, I've heard of people getting stuck with a problem, but this is ridiculous.

*He opens the downstairs bathroom door to go off.*

FLAVIA. I'm different, though. I quite like the odd surprise in life.

*A pane of glass drops neatly out of the mullioned window, and an arm comes through and releases the catch.*

MRS CLACKETT. That's good. Because now we're being burgled.

*The window opens, and through it appears the* BURGLAR, *played by* TIM.

BURGLAR. No bars. No burglar alarms. They ought to be prosecuted for incitement.

*He climbs in, and looks round in surprise to find the room full of people.*

MRS CLACKETT. Come in and join the party, love.

BURGLAR (*uncertainly*): No, but sometimes it makes me want to sit down and weep.

MRS CLACKETT. That's how we all feel.

PHILIP. Oh, Great Scott.

FLAVIA. No, this is most exciting! I've never met a burglar before!

ROGER. We just stand here and, I mean, what, we help him carry it out?

PHILIP. This is my fault.

FLAVIA. No, we can ask him about his work!

PHILIP. I'm terribly sorry. Because when I say: 'I've heard of people getting stuck with a problem, but this is ridiculous,' and I open this door . . .

*He opens the downstairs bathroom again.*
*A pane of glass drops neatly out of the mullioned window, and an arm comes through.*
*Enter through the window the* BURGLAR, *played by* SELSDON.

BURGLAR SELSDON. No bars. No burglar alarms. They ought to be prosecuted for incitement.

*He climbs in, becoming uneasily aware of the others as he does so.*

PHILIP. Oh dear, I've done it again.

BURGLAR. No, but sometimes it makes me want to sit down and weep.

MRS CLACKETT. I know, love, it's getting like a funeral in here.

ROGER. I mean, *now* what?

FLAVIA. We'll work something out.

BURGLAR SELSDON. When I think I used to do banks!

FLAVIA. Just keep going.

BURGLAR SELSDON *and* BURGLAR TIM (*together*): When I remember I used to do bullion vaults!

PHILIP. Oh dear oh dear oh dear.

THE TWO BURGLARS (*together*): What am I doing now? — I'm breaking into paper bags . . .

FLAVIA. Keep going.

BURGLAR SELSDON. Stop?

FLAVIA. No, no!

BURGLAR SELSDON. I thought the coast was clear, you see. I saw him going out to the bathroom.

FLAVIA (*closes the downstairs bathroom door*): It's all right. We'll think of something.

ROGER. They can't burgle the house now! Not two of them! Not with all of us standing here! I mean, be, you know.

MRS CLACKETT. What do you want them to do? Climb out and come back later?

BURGLAR SELSDON. Oh, no, I was listening most carefully. What's it he says?

PHILIP. 'I've heard of people getting stuck with a problem, but this is ridiculous.'

BURGLAR SELSDON. And he opened the door . . .

BURGLAR SELSDON *opens the downstairs bathroom door to demonstrate.*

BURGLAR SELSDON. So naturally . . .

*A pane of glass drops out of the mullioned window, and an arm comes through.*
*Enter through the window the* BURGLAR, *played by* LLOYD.

BURGLAR LLOYD. No bars. No burglar alarms. They ought to be prosecuted for incitement.

*He climbs in, very uncertain what's happening to him. He doesn't know whether to react to the presence of the others or not.*

PHILIP. Oh no!

MRS CLACKETT. They always come in threes, don't they.

ALL 3 BURGLARS. When I think I used to do banks! When I remember I used to do bullion vaults . . .

FLAVIA. Hold on! We know this man!

LLOYD. I've stepped off the edge of the world.

FLAVIA. He's not a burglar!

LLOYD. I just got here from the station.

FLAVIA. He's our social worker!

ROGER. He's *what*?

FLAVIA. He's that nice man who comes in and tells us what to do!

LLOYD (*dazed and uncomprehending*): So what am I doing? I'm stealing the TV? I'm fixing myself a drink?

FLAVIA. No, my love, you're helping us with our problems.

LLOYD. I've been working on Richard III for the last six weeks!

MRS CLACKETT. You think he needs working on more than we do?

LLOYD. I don't know where we are. I don't know where we're going.

FLAVIA. Here is where we are, my sweet. On is where we're going.

BURGLAR SELSDON. *He's* the burglar now, is he?

MRS CLACKETT. No, no.

BURGLAR SELSDON. Got the sack, have I?

FLAVIA. No, no, no!

LLOYD. OK. OK. I'll think of something. (*To* MRS CLACKETT:) Fetch the sardines!

MRS CLACKETT. I've fetched the sardines!

LLOYD. You've fetched the sardines?

OMNES. She's fetched the sardines!

PHILIP. Oh dear.

LLOYD (*to* PHILIP): Get the tax demand!

OMNES. He's got the tax demand!

LLOYD. You've got the tax demand. Hold on.

*He gives the whisky and glass to* FLAVIA, *and gets out his pills.* FLAVIA *pours him a glass.*

You've all met each other, have you?

OMNES. Yes!

LLOYD. Right, then, I suggest . . . (*Takes a pill.*) I suggest . . .

*FLAVIA hands him the glass of whisky to wash the pill down. ROGER and MRS CLACKETT signal him not to drink, but he drinks it all at one go.*

I suggest . . .

*He becomes unable to speak or breathe, and looks in amazement at the glass.*

FLAVIA (*sniffs the bottle*): It's the real one!

MRS CLACKETT. Who put that there?

BURGLAR SELSDON. We're doing it, are we?

FLAVIA. What?

BURGLAR SELSDON. Richard III?

LLOYD (*choked*): I can't speak!

MRS CLACKETT. What's he saying?

FLAVIA. He's saying . . . ring the police!

ROGER. Ring the police?

OMNES. Ring the police!

ROGER *picks up the receiver, finds the body of the phone is missing, and hands the receiver on to* LLOYD.

ROGER. It's for you.

LLOYD *puts the receiver to his ear and tries to dial.*

LLOYD (*faintly*): No phone!

FLAVIA. No phone?

MRS CLACKETT (*to* TIM): Fetch a phone!

TIM. Fetch a phone?

*Exit* TIM *through the front door.*

FLAVIA. Here's the phone!

ROGER (*hands* LLOYD *the phone*): We've found the phone!

LLOYD (*faintly, into the receiver*): We've found the phone! (*He puts the receiver back on top of the phone. At once it rings.*)

ROGER. What?

PHILIP. Oh dear. Oh dear. Oh dear.

FLAVIA (*to* PHILIP): Pull yourself together! (*To* LLOYD:) Pick it up!

LLOYD (*faintly*): Pick it up?

OMNES. Pick it up!

   LLOYD *picks it up hopelessly.*

MRS CLACKETT. Who is it?

FLAVIA. It's the police!

FLAVIA. Tell them . . . we're just missing a young woman!

ROGER. Yes! We're just missing a young woman!

   *Enter* VICKI *through the window.*

VICKI. It's in the garden now, and it's a man!

MRS CLACKETT. Oh, it's her! We'd forgotten all about her!

FLAVIA. So *that's* what's been going on! Our social worker has been doing his social work in the garden!

MRS CLACKETT. Oh, the crafty devil!

FLAVIA (*to* VICKI): So what do you say to *that*, my pet?

VICKI. No, he almost saw me!

MRS CLACKETT. What?

ROGER. It'll be 'The things are here' next.

VICKI. The things are here next.

FLAVIA (*to* VICKI): All right. (*To* LLOYD:) So what do you say to that, my sweet?

LLOYD (*faintly*): I've got to get the 8.40 back to London.

   LLOYD *opens the door to flee, but recoils, because there on the doorstep stands the* SHEIKH, *played by* POPPY.

MRS CLACKETT. Oh, it's the other one! And in her wedding dress!

OMNES. Oh!

POPPY (*uncertainly*): A house of heavenly peace . . .?

FLAVIA. Yes! Yes! It's their wedding day! What a happy ending!

OMNES. Ah!

LLOYD *and* POPPY *are hurriedly ushered down centre.*

MRS CLACKETT. And what does she say to that?

VICKI. Here are the sardines!

MRS CLACKETT. Never mind, love. (*Claps her on the back.*)
You can't see nothing.

*And indeed the clap on the back has dislodged* VICKI'*s
lenses.*

FLAVIA. They just want to be alone in their new home. If only
that window at the front had a curtain!

*Enter* TIM *through the downstairs bathroom, dressed in the
black sheets.*

TIM. Curtain?

MRS CLACKETT. Oh, and here's the mother of the bride!

TIM. Sheet?

OMNES. Curtain!

*Exit* TIM *into the wings.*

BURGLAR SELSDON. Last line?

OMNES. Last line!

BURGLAR SELSDON. But I'll tell you one thing, Vicki.

*They all look at* VICKI. *She is looking for her lenses.*

OMNES. What's that, Dad?

BURGLAR SELSDON. When all around is strife and uncertainty,
there's nothing like . . . (*Takes the sardines.*) . . . a good old-
fashioned plate of

OMNES. Sardines!

**Curtain.**